A DIVER IN THE DARK

First edition
published in 2009 by

WOODFIELD PUBLISHING LTD
Bognor Regis ~ West Sussex ~ England ~ PO21 5EL
www.woodfieldpublishing.com

ISBN 1-84683-082-6

A Diver in the Dark

Experiences of a pioneer
Royal Navy Clearance Diver
and former diving partner to
Commander Lionel 'Buster' Crabb

SYDNEY KNOWLES

Woodfield

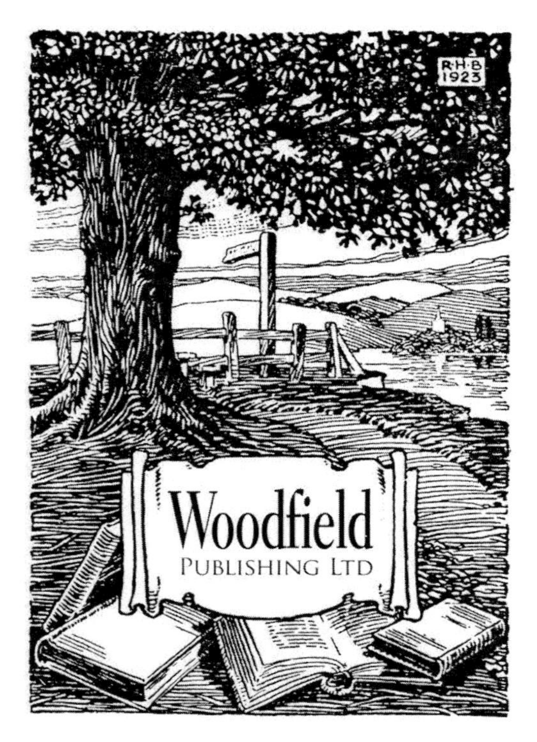

Woodfield Publishing Ltd

Woodfield House ~ Babsham Lane ~ Bognor Regis ~ West Sussex ~ PO21 5EL
telephone 01243 821234 ~ **e-mail** enquiries@woodfieldpublishing.co.uk

To the memory of my boss,
Commander Crabb RNVR, O.B.E., G.M.

And the many past and present Clearance Divers
throughout the world.

"Never break the neutrality of a port or place, but never consider as neutral any place from whence an attack is allowed to be made."

Horatio Nelson

~ CONTENTS ~

Acknowledgements

To Carol Kurrein for her proof-reading and creation of my web site.

To Ivor Howitt for supplying many of the photographs.

To George Gray for computer support.

And finally to many of my friends for encouraging me to write my memoirs, especially the members of the British Legion, Spain South.

Foreword

Sydney Knowles can be described as the hitherto 'silent partner' of the legendary diving officer, Commander Lionel 'Buster' Crabb OBE, GM, RNVR. As Crabb's assistant and confidant, he shared his wartime exploits against Italian underwater charioteers bent on sabotaging Allied ships at Gibraltar. Together, they also dealt with explosive booby traps in other Mediterranean ports and elsewhere, searched for Spanish treasure in Tobermory Bay and undertook clandestine missions under Soviet warships at the height of the Cold War. Rarely have tales of such derring-do appeared outside works of fiction.

As one of the last surviving forebears of today's Royal Navy Clearance Diving Branch, Sydney is an important figure in the heritage of this small, close-knit band of professionals. Little is heard about them, although they continue to perform bomb and mine disposal, among their other tasks, on land and under the sea on a daily basis throughout the world. The long list of honours and decorations awarded for their work at home and in the South Pacific, the Falklands, the Suez Canal, the Red Sea and the Arabian Gulf, as well as in Iraq and Afghanistan, speaks for itself.

Rob Hoole
Vice Chairman & Webmaster
RN Minewarfare & Clearance Diving Officers' Association

The Author

Sydney Knowles was born in Preston, Lancashire in 1921 and lived there until leaving home to join the Royal Navy in 1939. He saw active service in the Second World War, including the pursuit of the Bismarck and the 'Pedestal' convoy to Malta in 1942, which suffered heavy losses of ships and men.

His naval career took an even more dangerous turn when he joined a select group of divers tasked with removing mines from ships and clearing ports. He became a close colleague and friend to Commander Lionel Crabb, with whom he would undertake numerous wartime bomb disposal tasks and later be involved in espionage and the recovery of sunken Spanish treasure.

Now retired, he lives with his wife in Southern Spain.

Sydney Knowles, Spain 2009.

Prologue

At the time of writing the year is 2008, I am 87 years of age and feel it is time that I set the record straight with the true version of my early life and my time spent diving with Commander Lionel Crabb as a Royal Navy frogman and his 'buddy diver' during and after the war.

I was born in 1921, in a poor area of the Lancashire cotton-mill town of Preston. My mother worked as a weaver at a local mill and when I reached the age of seven I was allowed to accompany her each Saturday morning to the weaving shed, where I helped her to clean her looms. This task involved me crawling under each loom and, with a hand brush, clearing away all the cotton dust from under the machinery, for failure to do this could result in the cloth being spoiled by oil stains. The weaving sheds were crowded on Saturdays with other women and small boys of my age all doing the same thing. None of these women got paid any extra for this task. I was often asked to help other weavers with their looms, as some parts could only be reached by a tiny person like me. For this work I was usually given a penny, but occasionally I would only be given a halfpenny and would show my disapproval by displaying a protruding lower lip and a lowering of my eyebrows!

After cleaning the looms, one of my other jobs was to sweep the long alleyways between them. Anyone who remembers the Gracie Fields song *Sally Pride of our Alley* will now know what she may have been alluding to. The shed on Saturdays was very quiet, with no click-clack of the shuttles as they flew across the loom or the picking sticks that slammed into the shuttles, nor was there the very loud, continuous slap of the miles of leather belting that drove every loom from a very large steam-driven flywheel in the engine room hundreds of yards away.

On a normal working day the weaving shed was a very noisy place, but the women could still continue to converse by using pronounced silent movements of their lips and hand gestures – a method of conversation that in later years would come in very useful, as the relentless noise left many women absolutely deaf. My mother, who never seemed to be in good health, operated three looms, but the lady next to her – a buxom, healthy person – worked with six and made double my mother's wage. I could help make a few more pennies by 'kissing the shuttle' – that is, placing my lips to a hole at the end of the shuttle and, with a strong suction, bring an end of cotton through to attach to the main beam. Many hundreds were required daily and a stand-by heap was necessary for the continuous making of cloth. Until I got used to it, I would often swallow yards of cotton thread and later amaze my younger brother and other boys by fishing in my mouth for a loose end then, hand over hand, producing what seemed miles and miles of cotton.

On our way home from the mill, I and a gang of other boys would call in to a small corner shop to spend our hard-earned pennies on a glass of root beer to wash away the cotton fluff from our throats, a "gobstopper" toffee (plus one for my younger brother David) and maybe a comic.

One Saturday morning as I was leaving the mill, hand-in-hand with my mother, I was knocked down by a steam wagon that was leaving the factory laden with rolls of cloth. It had accidentally mounted the pavement and all I recall was lying on my back and looking up at a shower of red hot cinders as they fell over me from the fire box above. I was dragged clear and luckily only had slight burns to my face and hair, but I cried and screamed all the way home. In the confusion I lost a penny that I was holding in my hand, so no sweets for me that day – a sad result after all my labours.

My father worked on the railway as a plate-layer, a job involving the replacing of old worn-out railway lines with new ones. Most of his work was out in the countryside and he would set off from home with a couple of wire snares in his dinner basket, which he would lay at the mouth of rabbit holes he found on the railway embankment near to his work. If we were lucky this would result in rabbit pie for dinner.

Preston was (and still is) on the express main line from London Euston to Glasgow. One day my headmaster at Saint Mathews school, Mr Wilson, removed me from class and abruptly informed me that my father had been killed. Even though there was no love lost between my father and I, the shock brought tears to my eyes and I sobbed uncontrollably. But later this bad news turned out not to be true; he had been working with a gang of eight men when an express train had ploughed into them, killing six of them, but my father and one other man had survived. I recall that his wage was at that time two guineas a week.

I also recall from an early age that people who had to start work very early in the morning would be brought from their slumbers by a "knocker" – a man who carried a long bamboo pole that he placed against the upstairs window and rattled against the glass to ensure that the occupant would not be late for work and risk having a fine deducted from his or her wage. The knocker would have as many as 20 or 30 houses to visit each morning – I believe it cost two pence a knock per week. Also, until the end of the war in 1945 and for a few years afterwards, the gas lamps at the end of our street were lit and doused by a man carrying a long pole with a hook and a flame at the end of it.

The few conversations my father had with me as a child were of his World War One memories and his time in Gallipoli fighting the Turks. He served with the Royal Lancashire Regiment where he became a 'runner'. This entailed delivering orders from one part of the Front to the other, making the runners a prime target for enemy snipers but when he was gassed it put an end to this dangerous duty. He described his time there as "hell on earth" and while telling a story would often break down in floods of tears and I would cry too, for I could not understand what was happening, while my mother would attempt to console the both of us.

Before the Great War my mother had been engaged to my father's brother David, whose hobby was wrestling in the Greek and Roman style. I believe that he was very good at his chosen sport and represented his county of Lancashire, but sadly he was killed in France early in the war. My mother was a very gentle person who was very musical. She played the piano well and also had a lovely voice; she was also a member of the local church choir and had the great honour of being asked to sing solo one Sunday morning for a BBC radio broadcast from York Minster.

This was a great event in our street. The neighbours volunteered to look after my younger brother David and I and my father and mother left home at 5.30am to catch the early morning tram to the railway station (buses had not yet been introduced in Preston). I was very excited and proud while waiting to hear my mother's voice and sat in front of the radio in our neighbour's house with half the kids in the street, surrounded by lively chatter. I cannot remember what she sang but the adults all agreed that it was beautiful, while the kids, with great disappointment, said "Is that all?" and ran out to play. I cried and stared at the silent radio, disappointed that it was all over so quickly.

My mother died, from cancer of the womb, after a long and painful illness, leaving me and my eight-year-old brother to the not-so-tender mercies of my terrifyingly brutal, drunken father. A year after the loss of my mother I decided to run away from home, for I was terrified of my father. I had no money and no idea where I was going to go. I was dressed as all the boys of my age did in Preston in 1930s – in a simple wool jumper and short pants[1] and on my feet I wore a pair of Lancashire clogs. This escapade was very

[1] I had not yet been "lengthened" – when boys became old enough to wear long pants – which in Preston at that time occurred only when boys had left school and found a job.

short-lived, for I had no food or shelter and, after walking about ten miles in the pouring rain, I found myself in the village of Longridge, where I knew that my schoolmaster, Mr Washington, lived. I sought him out and, after a severe reprimand from him, his wife put me into a hot tub. After giving me a meal the police were contacted and I was turned over to a policeman who arrived on a motorcycle with sidecar.

I told the policeman that I had run away from home because my father was always hitting me.

"You should be a good boy then," he said, and promptly put me in the sidecar and took me home. The policeman spoke to my father for a considerable time while they drank a number of bottles of beer and this must have put my Father in a good mood as I was not punished.

The Author's parents.

There were some happy days in the summer when the schools were closed for holidays. I would go with my friends down to the river Ribble and it was there that I first learned to swim, in an area known as Melling's Deeps. This was not the best place to learn to swim because the banks were full of tree roots that protruded into the river. The water was also very dark green and deep but one day I summoned up enough courage to leap in and, on coming to the surface, headed for the bank, doing a doggy paddle.

On another occasion, along with my best friend Harry Brown, we waded through a stream called 'Besser Brook' to raid a farmers potato field. On our return we made a fire and roasted the potatoes. Unfortunately, my new flannel trousers, which had become so dirty that I attempted to wash them in the stream, caught alight when I tried to dry them by placing them too close to the fire. I knew that my return home with one trouser leg missing would result in another thrashing from my father (and it did).

Another favourite pastime for Harry and I was to hunt for rabbits. I owned a whippet dog called Flash and very early Sunday morning, just as the sun was rising, Harry would come to my home and throw gravel at my window to wake me, which was my cue to wrap Flash in a bedsheet and lower him from the bedroom window. I would shin down the adjacent drainpipe and we would run off to the fields and woods to hunt for rabbits.

My brother David, four years my junior, would want to accompany me on all these excursions but, as anyone who has a younger brother would know, to have had him along would have hampered our fun. I never had a close relationship with him or appreciated him until we met up at the end of the war and had an emotional reunion in Portsmouth. He had joined the Royal Navy and was serving on Motor Torpedo Boats. The manner of our meeting was amazing. A group of sailors were playing darts in a pub that I and a shipmate had called into for a quick beer. While standing at the bar I heard one of the darts group shout "That was a very good bull – a great shot, Dave". I casually turned to look, and to my amazement and joy saw my brother David, who I had not seen for over four years. When I had left Preston my brother had still been at school. Now he was a grown man – and very smart he looked in his navy uniform.

A great annual event that the children of Preston looked forward to was the Cooperative Society Field Day, when literally thousands of local children and their parents gathered in Moor Park, adjacent to the Preston North End football ground. Every child had to take their own white enamel mug, which the Co-op staff filled with tea brewed in great tea urns and each child was given a large slab of 'parkin' (a type of gingerbread). Games were organised – skipping for the girls, wheelbarrow races for the boys, egg and spoon races, three-legged races and the like. In the centre of the park near the duck pond was a bandstand where the Co-op brass band played all day. The park was overflowing with noise and laughter and the mayor and organisers had to use a megaphone to be heard over the din. A horse pulling a wagonet that could seat about twelve gave children rides around the park at a penny a ride and this money was later given to the Red Cross.

Nearly every household shopped at the Co-op and collected their dividend or "divvy" stamps when goods were purchased. The amount of stamps you received depended on how much you spent. These stamps were licked and placed on a "divvy sheet" that was usually hung behind a cupboard door in the kitchen. When "divvy day" came around they were exchanged for money or goods.

Another grand event was when the Bertram Mills Circus came to town and my cousin Ida, who was a showgirl in the circus, took me around to see the wild animals and the various acts. She shared a caravan with five other girls and I thought this way of life must be wonderful and decided to run away again and join the circus. I made an attempt to follow them when they moved on but was apprehended in

Wigan and was again sent home – to receive a number of sharp clips round the ear from my father.

At the age of fourteen I left school and managed to survive the next four years doing a variety of jobs. I also looked after my younger brother and did the daily household chores, as dictated by my father. These tasks would involve having to clean the grate, lay the fire, make the beds and set the table for the evening meal. I used to have the radio on and remember listening to Henry Hall and the BBC orchestra.

My first job on leaving school was working for a fruit and vegetable merchant. Each morning my father would wake me at four thirty and I would set off to were Dolly the horse was stabled – a walk of a couple of miles. On arriving I would harness her to a cart and we would proceed to the distribution market in the centre of Preston to pick up our load of potatoes, cabbages and other vegetables, which we then transported to the small fruit and vegetable shop of Mr Wignall, my boss and Dolly's owner. There was very little traffic on the roads in those days and I recall the sound of Dolly's hooves echoing in the still morning air as we passed the high walls of the cotton mills. The best part of this job was the time I spent with Dolly. Mr Wignall was not the kindest of men and when he wasn't looking I would sneak extra bran for her. I was paid seven shillings and sixpence a week.

I then went to work repairing tarpaulin sheets, where I spent hours on my knees with a 'palm' (a leather pad held in the palm of the hand) and a shaped needle, sewing up rents in tarpaulin sheets. The stitching was then painted over with black bitumen. For this I received ten shillings for five and a half days' work.

I later worked in a brick-yard, wheeling coal slag (very fine coal dust), which was used for the baking of the bricks. It was very hard work but helped to harden my youthful body. I was jet black by the end of the day. At lunchtime I would often run errands to the local shops for my boss and I remember a shilling would buy for him a packet of twenty "Capstan Full Strength" cigarettes. Eventually my father complained about the amount of money it was costing to heat the water for my daily baths, so I changed jobs and went to work in a paper mill, where I earned sixteen shillings for twelve hour days and eighteen shillings for the night shift. I was a "picker scraper", which involved scraping the old wet pulp off the felts that carried the fresh pulp through the drying rollers and which would eventually become the finished paper.

Before I went to work in the paper mill, I would have to rush home to do all my chores and would dread the sound of my father's clogs out in the street, especially if he was drunk, as I knew this would mean another beating if everything at home wasn't the way he wanted it. One discipline he insisted upon was that until my brother and I had left school and started work we had to stand at the table for our meals. A fried egg was always cut in half between David and I and we were not allowed to speak until spoken to. When my mother was alive she often protested over this cruel ritual, but now we had no one to protest for us.

My first encounter with the opposite sex was a date at the Carlton Cinema with a girl called Patricia Pritt. It was the opening night of this new cinema and I was out to impress her, so I paid nine pence each for balcony seats. The film was *King Kong* starring Fay Wray. To further impress Patricia I invited her at the interval to an ice cream, knowing I had sixpence left. She was delighted and opened the tub promptly and tasted it but when the usherette asked for the sixpence, to my horror I discovered, after searching frantically in all my pockets, that I had lost it. This started loud giggles from other boys and girls seated nearby. Patricia was not impressed and stormed out of the cinema in a flood of tears shouting "You… I never want to see you again! You've embarrassed me!"

It was many years before I became involved again with the opposite sex and I never saw Patricia again. (Incidentally, I promised the manager I would bring the sixpence when I got paid the following week.)

My eighteenth birthday was on September 3rd 1939, the day that World War Two broke out and, seeing this as my means of escape from home and my brutal father, I joined the Royal Navy that very day without being called up. Most people thought I was very patriotic and I let them think that, never telling anyone the real reason.

This decision was to completely change my life and not in my wildest imagination could I have, at that time, known where it would lead me...

1. Action Stations in the Atlantic and Mediterranean

The North Atlantic, May 1941. It is 5.30am. I am sitting on the cold steel deck of an ammunition room aboard HMS *Zulu*, a Tribal Class destroyer, and surrounding me are racks of 4.7 inch shells. I had joined the Royal Navy on the 3rd of September 1939 – the day the war broke out – and since then had spent most of my service on convoy duty or U-Boat patrol in the North Atlantic. This is my Action Station and I am an ammunition loader when we are at action. My job is to send up, on demand, the shells required for the guns on the upper deck above me. Under normal conditions I would be down in the boiler or engine room, for my official title is First Class Stoker. In front of me lie the crumpled remains of my last meal, a ship's biscuit, as hard as the steel I am sitting on. 'The biscuit' has been served to crews in the navy for hundreds of years in an emergency or when a ship has run out of food. I believe that, many years ago, most of the biscuits were riddled with weevils, although fortunately not the ones I had recently been attempting to eat. This was the only food that the whole ship's company had eaten since the morning before, because under the conditions we were sailing it would have been impossible to cook and highly dangerous in the heaving galley.

We had just left Scapa Flow in the Orkneys where, having been given eight hours shore leave, I had taken a walk along a very barren shoreline and come across a small, isolated building with a welcome sign above the door. I was greeted by a very jovial gentleman who introduced himself as Tubby Clayton, the founder of TOC H, known worldwide as a place where servicemen could relax, away from military discipline, and be greeted by a friendly face. I had a long chat with him about my home life and a lovely cup of home-brewed tea. After a fond farewell, I returned to my ship.

We were now sailing north to Reykjavik, the capital of Iceland, to patrol the Denmark Straits. Cruising very slowly through thickening ice we saw, perched upon the ice, vast flocks of small brown birds. They took no notice of our presence until almost touched by our bow. We pressed on, hunting for U-boats and then suddenly were called to action stations. Without warning, our ship burst into speed and I was almost slung across the deck by the motion. We had changed course and were travelling at high speed through a stormy sea, in an attempt to overtake the German Battleship *Bismarck*, which, some hours earlier had shelled and, to our dismay, sunk the pride of the Royal Navy, the great battleship HMS *Hood*, with the loss of over 1,000 lives. I was now below decks at my action station. Before and above me was the steel hatch and ladder I had descended some hours earlier. If we were to be sunk, I prayed that I would go in a blinding flash and not be trapped below, for my only means of escape was through that hatch, which could only be opened from outside.

It is well documented that the *Bismarck* was eventually caught and sunk by our capital ships and our revenge accomplished.

A thousand white horses flecked with blood,
At the sinking of the Hood
So much death so much gore,
What an awful bloody war!
Shot and shell must now fall,
Against Bismarck's iron wall.
And all now must abide,
Till we revenge the men that died.
So now more death, now more gore,
What an awful bloody war!

Stoker, Syd 'Baron' Knowles
Denmark Straits, North Atlantic, May 1941

My mind was taken back vividly to December 14th 1940, when I was wounded in the chest and my jaw broken in action, at Trondheim in Norway, where our Tribal Flotilla had damaged a number of German destroyers in what our captain described as ‘a skirmish’. I was one of the lucky ones, for one of my shipmates on the upper deck, whose action station was at the torpedo tubes, had been killed. Many more, like myself, had been wounded.

The Author when a crewmember of HMS Zulu, 1941.

My station at that time had been Engineer’s Writer. My duty was to follow the Engineer Officer closely during action and convey any message he issued to various parts of the ship. When running aft along the upper deck with a message I was hit by shrapnel when a shell struck our searchlight platform nearby.

I was admitted to the ship’s sickbay and at the first port of call was transferred to a Scottish hospital in Ballochmyle, north of Glasgow, which had previously been a stately home.

There I was placed under the skilful care of Sister Black, a real disciplinarian and a wonderful person, whom I shall never forget. I had to take my food as liquids through a tube because I had broken my jaw and it was gripped together with gold wire. I could have felt sorry for myself until I looked around at others in the ward, they being mainly RAF pilots who were suffering from very severe facial burns. One, a Norwegian fighter pilot, explained that when he was shot down he had had difficulty releasing his seat belt before escaping from the blazing cockpit to bail out.

I soon recovered, minus all of my teeth and thus have been forced to wear full dentures ever since the age of eighteen. I can recommend it; no more visits to the dentist for the rest of your life! After discharge from the hospital I rejoined my depot, HMS *Drake* in Devonport. I never saw my old ship HMS *Zulu* again, for she was sunk, after striking a mine, at Tobruk in North Africa some years later.

HMS Zulu.

The next ship I was drafted to, after a couple of months at the barracks of HMS *Drake* was a destroyer, HMS *Lookout*.

We are now at sea in the Atlantic, south of Ireland and with our sister ship HMS *Lafore* we are on our way south to join up with 'Harpoon', the name of the convoy from Halifax, Nova Scotia, on its way to Malta.

My rank now is First Class Stoker Mechanic and, along with the other 22 Boiler and Engine Room personnel, I was crammed into a Mess deck measuring 6 x 7 metres. This was where we slept, ate and lived, under our swaying hammocks. Sometimes the air circulator worked, but a urinal would better describe the stench and taste of the air we had to breathe, although I always felt sorry for the crews of submarines, who sailed in far worse conditions than we.

I vividly recall my first sight of Gibraltar on the port bow as we entered the Mediterranean. This massive white rock would eventually play a very important part in my life. After entering the port and refuelling, we sailed east on our way to Malta.

The next ten days can only be described as horrific, for we were at action stations for six days and nights, along with other escort vessels, in an attempt to beat off wave after wave of Italian and German dive-bombers, determined that our supply ships – filled with food, ammunition, petrol and other vital supplies – would not get to Malta. They almost succeeded, for a great number of our merchant ships and escorts were sunk. During most of this time, I was once again in my least favourite action station, the Ammunition room – and back on ship's biscuits.

Nearing Malta, we parted from the convoy and headed at high speed to Alexandria, to take on oil fuel, and from there on to the Suez Canal. Sailing through the canal is an amazing sight, with the desert stretching as far as the eye can see, yet almost brushing the ship's sides. Leaving the canal astern, we headed into the Red Sea and on to the port of Aden and the entrance to the Indian Ocean. Then, turning to starboard, we sailed almost due south to Mombasa for refuelling and then, after only two days in harbour, we sailed again to the south.

Whilst in both Aden and Mombasa, no shore leave was given and the "Buss" whispers of our destination were rife. Our captain then informed the crew that we were to be part of an invasion force of the island of Madagascar, to be called

Operation *Ironclad.* The island, at that time, was held by the Vichy French, who were pro-German.

It is now May 1942. We are anchored just off the port of Diego Suarez on the north-west coast of the island. We saw no action, nor heard a shot fired, but other members of the battle fleet, which included the old battleship HMS *Warspite,* did a first-class job and soon took control of the island further south.

Our job now complete in Diego Suarez, we leave Madagascar and head north to the Seychelles, a group of islands in British possession since 1810, where a lone oil tanker was anchored, awaiting any British vessel that passed her way. The crew of the tanker were almost insane with boredom. We gave them white bread and other stores that they sincerely appreciated, especially the rum.

Orders changed and instead of sailing down to Cape Town we headed on across the Indian Ocean to Colombo, Ceylon (now Sri Lanka) for a much-needed boiler clean, there being no other port available. To the joy of the whole ship's company, we were invited to take a trip into the mountains to an R&R (rest and relaxation) camp situated in the tea plantations of Bandorowela, in the central south of the island. We boarded a very rickety old steam train with wooden seats, which puffed its way up the mountain through jungle-like vegetation, which then opened up onto the terraces covered with regimented rows of tea plants, tended by native women wearing brightly coloured saris. During our ten-day stay we were invited to the homes of the plantation owners, most of whom were British ex-pats, and there we were made most welcome and invited for drinks (thankfully not tea).

Near to the R&R camp was a nine-hole golf course and I was invited to make up a foursome. I was amazed how very straight my companions drove off from the tee, until they informed me that they had played the course the day before and to their alarm had discovered that the rough held many snakes.

On our way back to the camp we had to cross a football pitch. It was almost evening and, in the gloom, I thought I could see a number of figures around the distant goalposts. We got a tremendous shock when we approached a coughing, snarling pack of baboons. I grasped a three wood, then thought better of it and ran for my life, followed by my partners and shocked curses of "F***ing hell! Go man, GO!"

After the poisonous snakes and snarling baboons I decided that perhaps we would be safer at sea.

We then returned to the capital Colombo, a city which I found to have two very different faces. Near to the port there was much poverty and child prostitution, of both sexes, being offered blatantly to sailors, but the city area was more affluent. Here there were lots of tiny jewellery shops displaying rings, brooches and necklaces, all made out of semi-precious stones from the local area. These could also be purchased from men on the street at an amazingly cheap price. I bought a moonstone necklace and bracelet, in the expectation of one day meeting the right girl to give them to. We were all, from the highest ranking officer down to the ordinary sailor, addressed as "Master" by the locals. There were little stalls, roofed with coconut leaves, selling bowls of rice and curry or the local drink, *arak*, distilled from coconut milk. When added to water it took on a milky colour and was very potent. The officers were entertained at the beautiful Galle Face Hotel, which was out of bounds to other ranks but who had the service of the wonderful Fleet Club at the rear of the hotel, set in tropical gardens overlooking the sea. I had not previously realised what a strong influence the Dutch had held over this part of the island, for it had been a trading centre for centuries and on the spice route to the Far East for sailing vessels.

Next stop Durban, to take on fuel oil. The view of the city from out at sea was wonderful, its tall white buildings shimmering in the sunlight. The whole ship's company were delighted when we were greeted by the famous *Lady in White* – Perla Siedle Gibson – who, at the age of 50, was standing on the jetty, dressed in her trademark flowing white dress and floppy red hat, singing to us in her wonderful operatic voice, as she did to all the war and troopships that entered the harbour.[2]

Finding that we would be in port for a number of days, we were given shore leave and I was surprised to see a great number of Zulu men with beautiful white feathers flowing from their hair doing what I thought was the degrading job of rickshaw pulling, for I believed them to be a very proud race.

Before sailing on to Cape Town and during our stay in Durban, one of the ship's company, Able Seaman 'Shiner' Wright, decided to desert the ship and a search for him proved unsuccessful. Many years later, during a conversation with a sailor in the Trocadero bar, Main Street, Gibraltar, I was amazed to discover that he had met 'Shiner', who was still living in Durban and now had a job as an inspector on the city tramway. Apparently he had at first got a job on a whaling ship but deserted again because he found it cruel and disgusting (I agree).

At Cape Town the view of Table Mountain from way out at sea was stunning. Again, we were granted leave and here, in the notorious District Six, I tasted my first Cape Plum Brandy, which, apart from its other effects, helped to warm me up, as I was feeling the cold after leaving the tropics. Cape Town in August was a very cold place, as it was their mid-winter.

Leaving Cape Town we headed north to Brazzaville, at the mouth of the Congo. Nearing the estuary we encountered a U-Boat. It was 4.15am and I had just finished the middle watch in the Boiler Room and returned to my hammock when the Action Station bell rang. There I was again, going

---

[2] It is believed that Perla Siedle Gibson sang 1,300 songs during the war, including 250 songs in one day when a large convoy arrived in Durban. She even sang on the day that she received news that her son had been killed in Italy. A plaque was placed on the jetty by the Royal Navy at the spot she sang from and, later, a wonderful statue of her was erected, which can still be seen at the Ocean Terminal.

down to that dreaded Ammunition room to spend many miserable hours, only broken by the tremendous roar of our depth charges. I am sorry to say that the U-boat slunk away.

We then went on to St Helena, the former island prison of Napoleon and the place of his death in 1821, a place very few people have visited. A party of us went ashore and I remember climbing up a few hundred steps to a small building that had been Napoleon's prison home. Little did I know that sometime later I was also to visit the island of Elba, off the west coast of northern Italy, where Napoleon was initially imprisoned and from where he later escaped.

North now, and on to Freetown, West Africa for refuelling. All ships that anchored there were visited by swarms of swimming naked children who called to the sailors on the ships above them to throw down coins into the water, where their shiny black bodies could be seen many feet under the surface, where the coins where deftly caught by them before sinking out of reach. "Glasgow Tanners," they called. "Throw Glasgow Tanners!" We happily threw all the loose change we possessed and then, leaving the poor but happy children behind, we sailed on to our final destination, Gibraltar.

Life on board small HM ships at that time was very different than today. For example, the only members of a ship's company to sleep in a bunk were officers, the rest of the crew having to use hammocks, although in my opinion these were by far the more comfortable, especially in rough weather, when the hammock would swing smoothly from side to side while the occupants of the bunks would be lurched from one bodily position to the other, making sleep almost impossible. Space per person was at a premium too, with only those men going on watch being allowed at the mess deck table for meals, followed by the off-watch crew.

In today's Navy, the crew are fed in a dining mess and the menu is the same for all. On wartime destroyers there were several messes, and each catered for itself. Every week one man would act as duty caterer and be issued with food for his mess, which he would prepare daily and take to the galley to be cooked. One of my favourite meals was 'pot mess' when, at the end of the month, any tinned foods and other unused foods – which could include bread, fruit, corned beef, jam, sardines, bottles of HP sauce, baked beans and sausages – were all placed in a 'fanny' (a large pot) and boiled up. Sounds disgusting, I know, but by God it was good!

At 11am in the forenoon watch 'Up Spirits' was piped by the Quartermaster and on every mess deck the shouted response would be "Stand Fast The Holy Ghost!" and each mess would be issued with a tot of rum per man, approximately half a tumbler, which a sailor could either drink or unofficially use as a barter. Some men set up their own "firms", each of which had a specific name to describe the service provided – for example to "snob" (cobble shoes), "dobey" (wash clothing), "Jew" (mend clothing and stitch on badges) and "Sweeney" (barber). Each charged in rum for their services, so a basic rate, for instance, sewing on one button would be a "sipper," two or more buttons would be a "wet", washing an overall could cost a "gulper" and the resole of a pair of shoes might cost a "see-er off" or "sandy bottom" – in other words, the whole tot.

I feel very sorry for today's sailors, for the issue of 'grog' or Pusser's Rum, which was served on board ships of the Royal Navy for 330 years, is no longer in practise. The word Grog, was the nickname of Admiral Vernon, known by sailors as "Old Grog" from the "grogram" cloak he wore. These cloaks were made out of a coarse fabric of silk or mohair and wool, often stiffened with gum.

Readers may be interested to know a little of the history of Navy Rum. Only the Monarch can order "Splice the Main Brace!" whereupon every sailor that day receives a double tot. In 1970, the Admiralty Board decreed that there was no place for the daily issue of Pusser's Rum in a modern navy and so ended the daily issue of Pusser's Rum, on July 31st 1970, ever after referred to as "Black Tot Day" and on that day around the world, on every ship in the Royal Navy, glasses were raised in their final salute to "The Queen!" On very rare occasions her Majesty can still signal "Splice the Main Brace".

But the Pusser's Rum tradition is still alive. In 1979 Charles Tobias, entrepreneur and global sailor, obtained the rights and all the blending information from the Admiralty and formed Pusser's Ltd, on Tortola in the British Virgin Islands, so this genuine navy rum has been available to the public since 1980. Fortunately, I live in Southern Spain and close to Gibraltar, where I can purchase it. To keep up tradition, I partake of an occasional tot and toast "The Royal Navy" who gave me such a wonderful life, filled with so many adventures.

Personal hygiene was not difficult but different. For example, fresh water was always scarce, so we would sluice ourselves down from a tin bucket of water, which was then topped up and used to wash our clothes. We could also shower using seawater – as much as we wanted – using special saltwater soap. Almost all sailors smoked cigarettes and tobacco could be bought from the ship store in one-pound tins called "Tittlers" for one shilling (5p). Off watch, men would sit for hours at the mess deck table, hand-rolling their cigarettes and wrapping their great brown leaves of pipe tobacco (first sprinkled with rum) in canvas, which was then tightly lashed in cod-line to form a "prick". This would then be slung into a locker for use at least a year or so later when matured and ready for the pipe.

Contact with home and loved-ones was solely by letters, which had to be censored by a ship's officer, for reasons of security, it being vital that no one knew our location (although most of the time the crew had little idea where they were themselves!) Also, because mail took many months to be carried backwards and forwards to the UK, it was often the case that by the time a love letter was received by a girl back home, the recipient would already have been replaced by a new love! It's often true what they say about Jolly Jack Tars having a girl in every port!

2. Gibraltar and 'Pedestal'

After our circumnavigation of the continent of Africa we prepared HMS *Lookout* for our next possible encounter with the enemy, which was to be soon. The harbour and anchorage of Gibraltar was filling up with ships that included two battleships, four aircraft carriers, seven cruisers, 32 destroyers and many merchantmen. This was the launch of *Pedestal* – the great August 1942 convoy for the relief of Malta.

HMS Lookout.

We were soon engaged by the enemy, only a couple of days after leaving Gibraltar, when at dawn we were attacked by wave after wave of Italian and German dive-bombers. I was down again in my dreaded Ammunition Room and was soon joined by another crewmember to assist me with the loading of shells onto the hoist that fed the guns on the upper deck. In this steel-lined room the roar of the guns above us was horrendous and although each attack lasted only fifteen minutes or so as the separate waves of bombers swept over us, the guns fired non-stop and we were obliged to feed the hoists continuously to satisfy the demand.

We could feel our ship dodging and weaving its way through the exploding bombs and I thought we had been hit several times when the blasts hammered against the very thin sheets of the destroyer's hull. My companion was a very young Ordinary Seaman who had been called from his civilian life into this mayhem. He was a new member of the crew and this was his very first action. He voiced his fear at every explosion with shrill screams and sobs. Although I was as frightened as he, I put my arms around him in an effort to comfort him and gave to him a strict "talking to". This seemed to help him considerably and he bravely carried on his work of loading shells for the remainder of the furious action. The attacks went on hour after hour until sunset and we had to remain at action stations all through the night. Although we were completely exhausted, I found it impossible to sleep on the cold steel deck. I lay awake thinking of what was to come. The convoy was being attacked by over seven hundred aircraft in wave after wave and we fought like tigers.

I wasn't afraid of facing the enemy or danger but this steel box was a rat trap and I determined there and then that if I came out of this alive I would request a change of action stations. Then I remembered my normal job, a stoker. By rights I could have been down in the boiler room, another rat trap.

Early next morning I was relieved for a toilet visit and when returning along the upper deck I was ordered to take charge of a damage control fire pump beneath the searchlight platform. Its operator, John 'Snowy' White, a stoker and a mess-mate of mine, had just been killed, decapitated by a large piece of shrapnel. I was given a steel helmet and told that breakfast would be coming soon. The latter turned out to be couple of ship's biscuits, bone hard, and a boiling hot cup of kye, a hot and very nourishing chocolate drink, to be taken where we stood. I could not have stomached anything else, for I felt sick and shocked at the sight of a man I knew so well who was now just a piece of bloody gore. Snowy was buried at sea the following day.

Hardly had the sun broken over the horizon at our bow when the shrill sound of 'action stations' blasted our ears. I looked around for the familiar sight of a convoy, but what I saw was amazing – our ships spread horizon-to-horizon as far as the eye could see – aircraft carriers, battleships, cruisers, destroyers, minesweepers and long lines of merchantmen, plus two large tankers, the latter being especially closely guarded by three destroyers, for the petrol they carried was urgently needed by our aircraft on Malta.

Scarcely had we gnawed through our meagre victuals when the guns opened up on every ship and the entire sky was covered in black shell-bursts, with shrapnel and brass cartridge cases falling like hailstones upon every ship and splashing in the sea around us.

The enemy planes had returned.

The nearest large ship to us was the aircraft carrier HMS *Eagle*, which was transporting fighter planes in her hangar and on the flight deck above for the defence of Malta. Suddenly, I saw four large spouts of water rising up her starboard side, followed by tremendous explosions. She had been torpedoed by a U-Boat that had very skilfully and bravely penetrated the lines of the convoy. The tremendous roar was joined by ear-splitting blasts from our 4.7-inch guns fore and aft and the continuous, deafening, thud-thud of the pom-poms and the rattle of Oerlikon ack-ack (anti-aircraft) guns all around us – plus the clang of empty shell cases as they were ejected from our guns and landed on the steel deck from bow to stern. It was indeed a test of our endurance.

Moments later, we, as the closest ship, started firing our depth charges in a pattern at high speed as we sped towards the *Eagle* to render assistance. Suddenly she started to sink by the bow and to port the aircraft on her flight deck skidded down and into the sea, amongst them, unfortunately, many human figures, some of them pilots still in the cockpits. Many survivors floated off her as she plunged to the depths. They were easily discernible, for most of them still wore the white anti-flash cotton head and arm covers that everyone wore at action stations.

But we dared not stop to help, for that would present a stationary target to the U-Boats and bomber aircraft above. We hated to have to do this, but many ships had been lost trying to pick up survivors and we just had to hope that they would be helped by a ship way back in the rear of the convoy, aptly named "Tail End Charlie".

One of the saddest incidents I witnessed was a survivor who we had picked up during a lapse in the attacks who had been lying on the deck recovering. He staggered to his feet, took a couple of unsteady steps and fell overboard through the space in the guard rail from where he was previously saved. A quiet "man overboard" was called but was completely ignored. We had all become stoic and had started to treat death with indifference. This was when I began to question my belief in God, especially when I heard men screaming with pain and saw them swimming for their lives in flaming thick black oil, in the majority of cases not calling for God but for their mothers. I know that what I am about to say will be thought controversial but I believe that while God is the creator, a mother creates her child and is therefore the child's God. The only consolation I could find was that their mothers could not witness these horrific scenes. As for myself, I have re-lived them many, many times over the years and it still brings tears to my eyes and a catch to my breath now, as I write about it.

The enemy was now sweeping in and attacking in force; wave after wave of bombers with long, cylindrical torpedoes slung beneath them and followed by the frenzy and screams of lines of dive-bombers – Stukas – designed to terrify, a sound that I could never, ever forget. Out on the horizon astern of us, I saw and heard a tremendous explosion. The cruiser HMS *Manchester* had been attacked by Italian high-speed E-boats that could travel at almost forty knots. Their torpedoes had penetrated into the stern boiler room, killing all the stokers and ripped open the ship's side, into which the sea gushed and within minutes the great cruiser was listing at forty-five degrees. Although still afloat, her captain,

Harold Drew, ordered "Abandon Ship" and scuttled her. Many of her crew survived, having drifted in boats and rafts to the North African shore, where they were taken prisoner by Vichy French soldiers. Her captain was later involved in a very controversial enquiry, reference to him leaving and deliberately sinking his command, but to this day survivors swear that the ship was mortally wounded and have stood by their captain, who never commanded another ship, but went on to work ashore for the rest of the war at the Admiralty with Admiral Mountbatten.

That evening, as the sun died behind us in the west and we were nearing Malta, an order was received to put about and return to Gibraltar. The tankers *Ohio* and *Santa Elisa*, with their precious cargo of petrol, limped eastward, closely guarded by two destroyers, HMS *Penn* and HMS *Ledbury*, and also a battered Malta tug, all lashed to the *Ohio's* sides to keep her afloat long enough to keep her from sinking and enable her to crawl into Bighi Bay. Although she eventually sank at her moorings, her cargo was intact and enabled Malta's aircraft to begin strikes against Rommel's supply convoys once more. I had great admiration for the crews of the tankers, for they were living and working above thousands of gallons of petrol – in essence, a massive bomb.

In formation, we and the battered remains of our fleet licked our wounds and staggered back towards Gibraltar, still beating off persistent attacks from the enemy bombers. The next day we would bury our dead at sea, a ceremony that I had unfortunately witnessed too many times in the previous few years. We would doff our caps, bite our lips and salute them as the canvas-covered bodies, weighted down with a link of anchor chain, were slid over the ship's side from under our flag, the White Ensign that they had served so well then down into the depths. They had done more than their duty.

It is now well documented that the tankers sailed into Valletta on August 15th 1942 and it is remembered every year to this day by a service of remembrance held on the walls overlooking the harbour. It had been one hell of a battle and our losses were high – nine merchantmen, the aircraft carrier HMS *Eagle,* the cruisers HMS *Manchester* and HMS *Cairo,* plus the destroyer HMS *Foresight* and many, many good men who would never see their families and homes again.

But Malta could live on, and this was our victory.

3. Gibraltar with Lieutenant Crabb

Just a few days after returning to Gibraltar from the Operation *Pedestal* Malta convoy, I saw a notice on the ship's noticeboard which read: "Volunteers required for hazardous duties ashore". I wondered what could be more hazardous than the hell I had experienced on the Malta convoys – surely nothing ashore could equal that? – and maybe at last I could get away from my dreaded ammunition room. So I decided to apply. I was soon to discover, however, that it was a case of "out of the frying pan and into the fire"!

I was interviewed in a dockyard office by Lieutenants Crabb and Bailey, the bomb and mine disposal officers. Lieutenant Crabb was a man of medium build, but with a strong and wiry body. They explained that explosions had taken place under two merchant ships a couple of months previously and this had led to the belief that the shipping in the anchorage was being attacked by enemy frogmen.[3]

This type of operation and attack had taken place in December 1941, when the Italian 10th Flotilla had successfully sunk the battleships HMS *Valiant* and HMS *Queen Elizabeth* in Alexandria harbour and also badly damaged a large tanker. With three two-man torpedoes[4] just six men had changed the balance of power in the Mediterranean. This

[3] These were frogmen of Gruppa Gamma, the sub-surface commando frogman section of the Italian Navy's **10th Assault Vehicle Flotilla** or (**Decima Flottiglia** Mezzi d'Assalto) also known as **Decima Flottiglia MAS** or X MAS) created in 1941. The Tenth Flotilla recruited from their fighting Services and trained the men in two groups. The **Gruppa Gamma**, or swimming section, who dressed in rubber suits and were equipped with breathing gear with double oxygen bottles worn slung low over the stomach area and swim fins. This group was trained to tow small mines with neutral buoyancy and attach them, with delayed-action fuses, below the waterline of Allied ships. They also used two-man torpedoes with detachable noses containing 300 kilograms of explosive – a deadly bomb that could be attached, with its time-fuse set, under any Allied ship.

[4] These two man torpedoes were nicknamed *miales* (pigs) by the Italian frogmen.

action drew a tribute from Churchill to their "ingenuity and extraordinary courage".

I was asked if I could swim and if I would be interested in learning to become a diver. I had always secretly yearned to be a diver but had never had the chance before, so with great excitement and much trepidation, I, Sydney "Baron" Knowles, together with five others – including, to my surprise, another man from Preston, my home town (Joe 'Rattler' Morgan) – plus Petty Officer David 'Dinger' Bell, 'Taff' Thomas, 'Jock' Frazer and Chief Petty Officer Ralph Thorpe, became the Royal Navy Underwater Working Party – not a very glamorous title for such a hazardous job but one of which I eventually became very proud .

We were to become the very first Clearance Diving Party in the Royal Navy and I am proud to say that the tradition we started has been carried on to this present day by brave, tough, gritty and resolute divers (all of whom, of course, also have sweethearts, wives and families).

Chief Petty Officer Thorpe had just been put ashore from the destroyer HMS *Brilliant* as being unfit for sea service but he had previously been a trainer of submarine crews in the use of Davis Submerged Escape Apparatus (DSEA), exactly the same gear that we were using to dive with. His knowledge was invaluable to us and he was very happy to join our party but he altered our easygoing routine with an iron fist.

"You may be divers but first you are sailors in the Royal Navy and as such you will conduct yourselves," he commanded. He also insisted that we dress in our number one uniform each Sunday morning if we were free to do so for Divisions – and that also included Lieutenant Crabb. As a result, occasionally, smartly dressed, we marched into town to attend a service at the Cathedral, conducted by a "Devil Dodger" (a term used in the Royal Navy for any religious minister).

Our party at first lived aboard an old Napoleonic prison hulk renamed HMS *Cormorant,* which was tied alongside the harbour wall. Life aboard HMS *Cormorant* took us all back to pre-Trafalgar days, for we could only walk between decks in a very stooped posture due to the very low beams above us. Now that we had experienced to some degree what life was like in Admiral Nelson's navy, we felt nothing but praise for the sailors of those days and our party stood out like a sore thumb, for almost everyone sported a wound, scab or plaster on the forehead after simply forgetting to bend at the waist. What it was like on a rolling sea I can only imagine.

Later we all moved to live together in new quarters within the walls of Gibraltar, at Jumpers Bastion, just below Alameda Gardens, where today you can ride the cable car up to the top of the Rock, were you will find a café and wonderful views across the bay and the Straits of Gibraltar into North Africa.

We added to our number by taking in a stray dog, who we named 'Nina', who later gave birth to three pups. We also had two cats and Lieutenant Crabb's pet parrot. A very pleasant surprise to all of us was to discover that the rear door from our new mess led onto a tennis court and this helped to keep up our fitness, for we spent our few off-duty hours in competitions, especially against officers and men of the RAF and the Black Watch Regiment.

Our only equipment for diving was the Davis Submerged Escape Apparatus (DSEA), scrounged from submarines, which were designed for coming up to the surface to escape from sunken or damaged submarines rather than for going down.[5] We had no diving suits or fins at that time; we just wore swimming trunks and lead-weighted plimsolls. The only problem with this oxygen breathing apparatus was that

[5] The Davis Submerged Escape Apparatus (DSEA) was an early type of oxygen rebreather invented in 1910 by Sir Robert Davis of Siebe Gorman and Co Ltd. While intended primarily as an emergency escape apparatus for Royal Navy submarine crews, it was sometimes used for diving. A DSEA set comprised a rubber breathing/buoyancy bag, which contained a canister of barium hydroxide to scrub exhaled carbon dioxide and a steel pressure cylinder holding approximately 56 litres of oxygen at a pressure of 120 bar with a hand-operated valve.

below 30 feet oxygen under pressure can become poisonous, owing to the alteration in the body's metabolism.[6]

On the morning I joined, Lieutenant Crabb – a man with a bold nose, patches of sprouting hair high up on each cheek and sporting a superbly rich and curling red beard, together making him look very aggressive and resolute – announced:

"We are searching for mines under a couple of merchant ships this morning Knowles," adding that there was an element of danger in the job. He then threw a Davis Set at me, saying, "Try it on. Put that pipe in your mouth, turn that valve on the bottle when you want to breathe… and follow me." A short while later I was diving under a very large ship.

And that was how I started my career as a diver.

Lieutenant Crabb, Gibraltar WW2 (note Davis Escape Set).

[6] Although I exceeded this depth myself many times, mostly due to the weight of my gym shoes and the lack of oxygen, which between them tried to sink me down to the seabed. I often I had to tear them off and ditch them before swimming to the surface. Fortunately, I have only once been affected by oxygen poisoning.

It was the first time I had ever breathed underwater. As the surface of the sea crept past my goggles I experienced the most amazing colour of blue I had ever seen and the feeling of a new life crept through my body.

'This is for me,' I muttered to myself.

I was paid a complement by Lieutenant Crabb a couple of days after my first dive.

"Knowles," he said. "You are a natural, a bloody natural! But don't let it go to your head or you may drown."

I have tried to heed this warning in everything I have done throughout my life ever since – and especially underwater!

Within a few days I had gained confidence in myself and my breathing gear and after a week I was appointed 'duty diver'. The following week another member of the party would take over as duty diver; the changeover occurred every Sunday evening. The duty involved going aboard a motor launch (ML) every night at 11pm to patrol the anchorage outside the harbour. Most of these guard launches were commanded by a young Sub-Lieutenant RNVR and either he or the coxswain (usually a Petty Officer), in the dawn's half light, would choose a merchant ship under which the diver should search for possible limpet mines.

I never liked this particular dive in winter, because I was shaken from my sleep by the officer or coxswain, both usually dressed in thick duffel coats, with the usual comment of "It's dive time diver – and rather you than me mate!" This meant crawling from under a couple of Pusser's blankets, leaving a lovely warm bunk and within minutes, dressed only in swimming trunks, plunging into a very cold, dark sea. It was often the ship nearest to the Spanish shore, which could be as close as 400 metres, because the anchorage in Gibraltar was so overcrowded at that time with ships heading into the North Africa war zone.

In the early days of our Party searching the ships, if we found anything unusual we had to surface and the officer on the ML would send out a radio signal for Lieutenant Crabb. We would then back off from the possible explosion area until he arrived with the rest of our Party in the diving launch. Lieutenant Crabb would then dive, inspect the suspicious object and, if he confirmed it as a mine, would attempt to render it safe *in situ* or detach it from the ship's bilge keel and allow it to sink to the seabed.

This time-wasting practise had to cease when more Italian frogmen and two-man submarine operators of the Gruppa Gamma arrived and increased their attacks on our shipping. From then on, every diver of our Clearance Diving Party had to use his own initiative if he found something – by levering magnetic mines from the ship's hull with our diving knives or, if it was a floatation mine, stabbing its collar with the knife, allowing the mine to sink to the seabed. If and when a diver found a mine attached by clamps to the bilge keel or propellers he was advised to call for assistance from our boss, for invariably the object would be booby-trapped and Lieutenant Crabb was the only person in our group qualified to deal with this type of situation.

Italian two-man torpedo-type mini-submarine or 'miale' (painting by the Author)

This searching of every ship that entered our waters went on day and night by our unit and involved many hundreds of exhausting dives over many months and our usual cautious approach sometimes became reckless. Some of the ships gathering for a convoy to Malta and North Africa numbered as many as thirty to forty and if possible every one of them had to be searched before sailing. They included battleships, aircraft carriers and troopships packed with thousands of Allied soldiers who, while at anchor, would stupidly hang over the ships' rails, watching us at work in the cold sea, often whistling and shouting ribald comments, to which we would answer: "We are going under your bottom and you Pongos will have your arse examined whether you like it or not!" Little did they realise that our work was to save their lives and that we could never forget the sinking of those two Royal Navy battleships in Alexandria harbour.

I dived one morning in very good visibility to discover that the vessel I was searching did not contain a single rivet in her hull. I believe it was the very first of the new, all-welded Liberty Ships, a new type of freighter built by the Americans. From the laying of the keel to launching they took only half the time of a riveted vessel to construct.

Shipping at anchor packed the bay in front of the Rock and no more than 400 yards from the Spanish shore and the port of Algeciras across the bay. Allied ships stretched in lines often up to three miles long from east to west. The steamer *Willowdale* arrived from Huelva in the southwest of Spain and moored just outside the entrance to the port. She had just been loaded with oranges meant for the children in Britain, a fruit that many of them had never seen before. We searched her, as normal, and as Lieutenant Crabb dragged himself along the bilge keel, with his weighted gym shoes trailing below him, he discovered a long torpedo-shaped green mine about three feet long. It was attached to the bilge keel by three clamps and he saw that to the tail of the mine was attached a propeller. Apparently, as the ship moved through the water this propeller would turn to a predetermined setting and the mine would then explode when the ship was out in the Atlantic, giving the impression that it had been torpedoed by a U-Boat and giving no suspicion of the enemy attacks at Gibraltar.

Lieutenant Crabb attempted to unscrew the clamps but failed. Then Petty Officer David Bell decided to assist him and plunged into the sea to help. Between them it took over half an hour to release it. This included the two of them having to change the oxygen bottles of the DSEA breathing sets they wore because the oxygen content only lasted about 15 minutes when working hard.

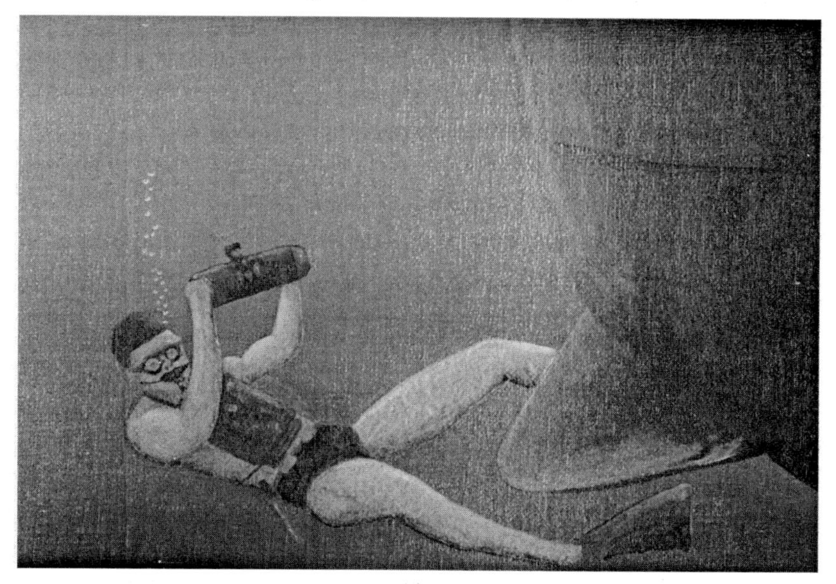

Removing a limpet mine (painting by the Author)

The Commander of the Port and Dockyard was Commander Hancock and he had great difficulty in finding a place to render the mine safe. When the mine was finally released it was taken away to the end of the runway, very close to two parked Spitfires, where it was rendered safe. This operation took a considerable amount of time, for this type of mine was unknown to us at the time. For this act of bravery, both Commander Crabb and Petty Officer David Bell were awarded the George Medal.

We later discovered that the operation to place the mine on the bilge keel of the *Willodale* was carried out in Spanish territorial waters at Huelva, while the ship was being loaded with oranges bound for Great Britain, by Friedrich Hummel, a German officer in the secret service and a German Wehrmacht specialist in underwater sabotage from a group called Marei-Marko Kampfschwimmers, who had been trained by the Italian Gruppa Gamma. Single-handed and equipped with simple German submarine escape apparatus DRAGER (similar to our DSEA breathing sets) and wearing a diving suit provided by the Italian Gruppa Gamma, he successfully placed the mine underwater onto the ship and watched her sail off to Gibraltar to take on oil fuel prior to leaving for Britain.

Diving operations of this type would be easy in Spanish ports, for no guards would be posted nor harbour waters patrolled, unlike Gibraltar, where security was very tight and depth charges were launched every few minutes.

In 1940, the German secret service *Abwehr* entered Spain with the task of seeing if it was possible to sabotage Gibraltar, but at that time it was strictly forbidden by the German High Command, although they did manage to recruit a number of Spanish workmen who worked for the British in Gibraltar dockyard and on the Rock. For most of the war Gibraltar was riddled with groups of Spanish fascists and communists willing to spy for the Germans and prepared to attempt sabotage on ships they were working on. The plan was to use an explosive with a delayed timer, which they intended to hide in the holds, so the ship would be sunk at sea, making the British think it had been torpedoed. The Spanish agents used by Hummel were simple workmen, who were told that if they carried out a sabotage job successfully they would receive a reward of 500,000 pesetas and a good job in Germany.

To provide labour for the fuelling of hundreds of ships in the dockyard, a convenient labour pool was very near at hand in the Spanish town of La Linea, just across the border.

It was from here that thousands of workers travelled daily into Gibraltar. All the Spanish workers, both men and women, had to return home each evening, after which the frontier gates would be locked for the night and an 11.30pm curfew enforced. This crossing of the military airfield, which was the only access to the Rock, created a tremendous security problem and a relatively easy channel for enemy agents to enter.

The bars and cafés of La Linea became favourite haunts of German agents seeking information about life in Gibraltar. During the Second World War three Spanish nationals were executed for spying: the first, in 1940, was Gibraltarian José Key, at Wandsworth Prison in London; eighteen months later Luis Lopez Cuenca, an agent working for the German Secret Service in Spain, was arrested for recruiting Spaniards who worked in Gibraltar to carry out acts of sabotage. Another Spaniard was arrested following an explosion on Coaling Island; he was Jose Martin Munoz, who was employed in the dockyard and sentenced to death by Chief Justice McDougall. The Home Office Executioner, Albert Pierrepoint, flew from England to perform the execution. Both men were buried on 11th January 1944 within Gibraltar's civil prison walls.

Today thousands of tourists enter Gibraltar every day by car, coach or on foot; they still have to cross the runway, which is now regulated by traffic lights. Spanish and Gibraltar police and customs have checkpoints at each end of the border and it is necessary to produce a passport.

We patrolled the ships at anchor by diving launch and at night our searchlight swept the surface of the sea and the sides of the ships. None of us had been to the Royal Navy diving school or passed the diving test, except PO Bell, and, apart from Lieutenant Crabb, none of our party had been given mine disposal training, nor did we have any proper diving gear compared to the enemy, who had rubber suits, fins and superior breathing apparatus.

I had, by now, begun to greatly admire my boss, who, by example, was not only a fearless leader but also a father figure to us all. He would enquire about our families, look with interest at our photographs and state that he was looking forward to meeting them all one day. We dived day and night, summer and winter, in temperatures as low as 8 degrees C and on some lengthy dives in winter it became mind numbing, dressed only in swimming trunks and with lead weights in our oversized gym shoes, hardly the ideal diving gear, which made us swim upright with a laboured dead-foot breast stroke. At each ship we would plunge into the sea and, well below the water line, grasp the bilge-keel that ran along the ship. We then pulled our way along it towards the stern, searching all the time for limpet mines or anything unusual. It was tough work, for we did not, at that time, have fins – or even know of their very existence![7] At the end of the bilge-keel it became a frantic and laboured swim to reach the rudder and propeller, which we could see in the distance and above which our diving boat waited to pick us up. At times the sheer exhaustion of swimming in this manner would cause the weights in our gym shoes to sink us down fathoms below the ship and on a number of occasions I had to tear them off and let them sink to the seabed then shoot to the surface "on a lung and a prayer".

Our crude method of pulling ourselves along the bilge keels resulted in all of us having our hands cut and torn on the barnacles adhering to the hulls, especially in rough weather, when we were thrown around by the swell. We were often cut from head to foot, our injuries sometimes turning septic. One very bad experience was when "Rattler" and I, while searching a merchant ship, found ourselves engulfed in a shoal of stinging jellyfish, which resulted in the whole of our bodies being covered in vivid red wheals, which were extremely painful. We were treated in the Naval Hospital, where we had to be washed down with some type of spirit – an experience I would not care to repeat!

[7] Later, we were to discover that the Italian frogmen had used fins for years, proving that the Italian diving equipment was the best in the world at that time.

"Rattler" became excited at the prospect of being treated in his nude state by one of the very few nurses based on the Rock but to his great disappointment in walked a male Sick Berth "tiffy" (a nickname given to all male nurses).

Equally excruciating was the intense cold we experienced between one dive and another. The majority of our dives were during the night, when temperatures fell, especially in mid-winter, when sitting shivering in the small diving launch in just our trunks with a thin towel over our shoulders for anything up to 30 minutes we suffered with terrible cramp in our limbs before we got to the next ship. We found it was a great relief to plunge into the sea again, which felt warmer than the cold air.

The climate of Gibraltar is described by the Central Office of Information as "mild and temperate during the winter months" but the sea temperature is usually around 40 degrees F and we took to wearing 'long johns' (ankle-length underpants) and heavy white woollen sweaters, but these proved to be useless when emerging from the water, for the sodden wool was very heavy and clumsy. After many hours of immersion through hours and hours of a long night's searching of ships and the bitter cold that we experienced, we became very fatigued and I found parts of my body disabled because of the violent shivering that came over us and many times found ourselves in the first stages of hypothermia. Jock Fraser commented that Captain Webb, who swam the English Channel, was covered in lard, but all we were covered in was goosepimples! At times we even found it difficult to speak and every time we surfaced and climbed into our diving launch we made a mad scramble to sit on the hot engine casing in an attempt to warm up.

We also found deep red furrows around our eyes, where the red rubber underwater goggles had bitten into our faces after many hours of wear and pressure. Commander Crabb seemed to suffer these problems most of all, but never ever complained and set an example to all of us, even when it was obvious that he was suffering excessive fatigue. He was a remarkable man.

We all looked forward to the welcome sign of dawn breaking and our return to the mess in Jumpers Bastion for hot food and a long, body-warming sleep.

During an emergency one night, I was in our diving launch on the port side of a large American Merchantman when a violent explosion took place on the starboard side, just below where PO David Bell was preparing to dive and search the ship's bottom. Amazingly "Dinger" was almost unhurt, except that a trickle of blood ran down his face from a splinter that had struck him just under the eye. His only comment was, "That's one less mine to search for!" A little later we dived in to see what damage had been inflicted on the ship and while below discovered another mine clamped menacingly onto the rudder post. It had not activated because the explosion of the first mine had stopped the time clock, which was most unusual, for normally it would have exploded sympathetically. We had not the time or knowledge for rendering it safe so it was removed and sunk in deep water for safety. I never heard it explode.

The Italians had invented a mine that was screwed to the bilge keel in such a way that it could not be removed without blowing up. Our answer to this was to cut off the area of bilge keel that it was attached to. This was my introduction to diving in the old standard diving helmet, borrowed from the Gibraltar dockyard. Wearing this gear we could operate an oxyacetylene underwater cutting torch that would allow us to remove the mine safely, plus the portion of the bilge keel to which it was attached.

I do not think that small air compressors had been invented at that time and we found it impossible and very exhausting work on the hand pump to supply air to both a diver and the envelope of the flame at the end of the cutting torch; this we improvised by using large cylinders of compressed air from the ship's deck above.

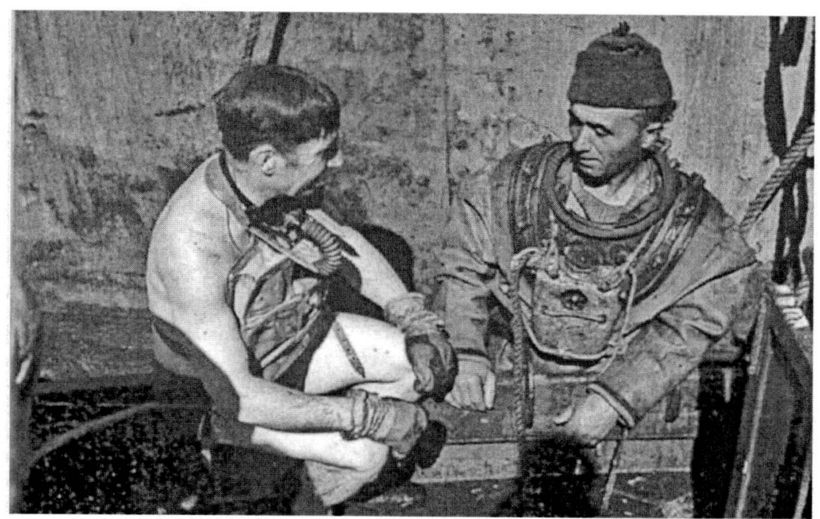

The Author and Lt Crabb, cutting a bilge keel, Gibraltar, WW2.

Royal Navy orders stated that only Mine and Bomb Disposal Officers were allowed to handle a mine but, due to our workload, we had to ignore this order, especially as Lieutenant Crabb was now working alone because Lieutenant Bailey had broken his ankle going down a ship's ladder and was no longer with our unit. He had been ordered back to Britain and was later to distinguish himself in the P-Party that cleared mines and bombs in Caen, France after D-Day, while under shellfire.

The very first mine I found was held to the ship's bottom by an inflatable rubber ring; a type that the Italians called a 'bug'. This type of mine was actuated by snapping a 'pencil' that contained acid that burned through to the detonator and exploded the mine. I was on a night dive and I had bumped into it as I laboriously swam in my heavy lead-weighted gym shoes along the ship's hull, groping in the dark. The moment I touched it I felt the beat of my heart stop and every fibre in my body froze. I was momentarily afraid and there followed a bewildering few minutes before I came to terms with the situation and rose, trembling, to the surface to inform Lieutenant Crabb, only to find that he had left in a second launch to search a ship that had signalled an emergency. By the time I could have contacted him the mine may have exploded and sunk or badly damaged the ship, so, taking very deep breaths of my neat oxygen, I recovered my sense, dived again and stabbed the inflatable ring with my army commando knife, which we had been issued to use while diving. I let the mine sink to the seabed, where it later exploded.[8]

I found my first night dive a very strange and weird sensation (and not at all like the kind of 'grope in the dark' I would have preferred to experience!) In the complete blackness, my mind wandered ahead of me and I imagined all sorts of things in front of me, especially when near the ship's engine room cooling water intake grill. I wondered if I could be sucked onto the grill and held fast until my oxygen supply ran out or my lungs were empty.

Underwater lights or torches had not yet come into use and all searches were confined to touch. I was amazed, however, at the wonderful colours and designs that my underwater movements made in the flashes of phosphorescence in the seawater around my body.

When we declared a ship as being 'clear', we often had our fingers crossed, hoping we had not missed anything. I asked my diving colleagues how they had felt on discovering their first mine and the answer was "just the same as you".

The same night, on another ship, I discovered a limpet mine clamped to the bilge-keel. It was easy to find, because I could hear the very loud ticking of its time-clock, which was only a few arm lengths from me. In the dark it sounded like the beating of a drum. I felt for it, then furiously unscrewed the clamp, tore it off and let it sink to the bottom, where it exploded some thirty minutes later. By that time I had been reunited with my boss, who calmly stated, "That's *your* mine

[8] It was only later, at the end of the war, when I had to return to Plymouth to take a course in Standard Diving, that I was issued with a Royal Navy diving knife in its heavy brass sheath.

Knowles." Before I could answer he put a firm, reassuring hand upon my shoulder and gave wink and a nod of satisfaction. I will never forget that dreaded "tick, tick, tick" as I dragged myself along the bilge keel towards it and I recall shouting into my mouthpiece "Don't stop! Don't stop!" I really was afraid. (I have yet to meet a diver who at some stage in his career has not felt the same and I would never buddy a diver in our type of work who stated that he was never afraid, for he would not be fully aware of his surroundings.)

It became very obvious to our party that we would have to ignore Royal Navy orders that only officers could handle mines if we were to save more ships. In any case, Lieutenant Crabb had a total dislike of rules for rules' sake and especially if they interfered with our progress. The Underwater Working Party lived a retired life of its own and we became resistant to any kind of influence from outside. Our work was our sole concern and we were all linked together by a tie more binding than formal discipline. We often found that after a very exhausting period of diving and living on our nerves and all sharing the action, we cared very much for each other and could almost speak to our officers man to man, yet still maintain discipline. We had become a "band of brothers" forged by trust, our mutual love of the work, and not least the frequent adrenalin rushes.

At one point, sitting alone one evening off duty, my mind began to wander – helped by the number of drinks I had taken – and I became maudlin. 'What the hell am I doing this job for?' I thought. 'I must be bloody crazy!' I was missing all my chances of promotion in the engineering branch I had joined. Thousands of people during the war simply hoped they would come through it alive and return to their families and here I was, jousting with danger day after day. I awoke the following morning, still at the table, with my head in my arms. I decided to speak to Lieutenant Crabb about my feelings and told him that was seriously considering leaving the Party and returning to General Service, so that I could try for promotion. He assured me that he would obtain a 'field promotion' for me as soon as possible, but he never did. He knew that promotion would take me away from the unit and he had other plans for me. (One could not be promoted within the Diving Group in those early days.)

Meanwhile, most of our time off duty was taken up by the boring and very strenuous work of topping up our used oxygen bottles from a very large cylinder by the use of a hand booster pump and replacing the Protosorb CO^2 granules that absorbed our exhaled breath and carbon dioxide, allowing us to re-breath clean oxygen.

At our mess in Jumpers Bastion we were visited one day by two military gentlemen from the department of psychiatry, one of them a naval doctor with a red stripe showing between his two and a half gold stripes and his partner, an army major. They stated that our diving team was perfect for analysis and proceeded to question our sanity.

"Do you have any trouble sleeping?" they asked, which was answered by, "Yes sir, we don't get enough and a woman or two would help!"

"How old were you when you could tell the time?" they continued, and "What do you reply to people who say that you must be crazy for doing the work that you do" and "Why do you do it and do you ever feel suicidal?"

To that question, we simply shrugged our shoulders. What they made of us I do not know, but as they were leaving the doctor turned and quietly said: "We admire your fortitude and we wish you well but your request for women is an impossibility here on the Rock. He then paused, turned and quietly said with a grin, "Maybe you are all crazy".

Over the years, I have often been asked if any of the actions that I went through return to my mind and I can honestly say, yes, continuously, as my wife can verify by the number of times I have frightened her by my nighttime shouts of warning or by waking from my sleep gasping for breath as I swim to the surface in my dreams. Yes, my war has left me with permanent scars.

False alarms came regularly, day and night, and many more mines where discovered. One night a large attack took place when Italian frogmen swam into the anchorage of Gibraltar, each of the twelve swimmers towing floating mines. They damaged the SS *Meta, Shuma, Empire Snipe* and *Baron Douglas* – so from the Italian point of view, the attack was a complete success. It had become impossible for our small diving group to search underneath every ship at anchor. Most of the mines we discovered were the bug type that adhered to the ship's bottom by floatation collars and which had been placed there by the swimmers of the Italian Gruppa Gamma.

Early one morning, a report came from a War Department ship that was anchored out in the bay and loaded with ammunitions and explosives, that the crew were about to abandon ship. The Captain stated that they could hear ticking from below the water underneath them. We raced out to dive and examine the bottom of the ship, but no mine could be found, although the ticking was still insistent and very audible, especially underwater. We went inboard and down into the engine-room and into the bilges from under the deck-plates, and the sound was still very clear. We had just entered the cargo hold and were about to search among the great stacks of ammunition boxes and explosives when from above PO Bell shouted that he had found the source of the ticking. Further down the line of anchored ships and a couple of hundred yards away, a salvage vessel was at work, using her large pumps and the ticking noise was created by their action. Sound underwater is very distinct and is five times louder than on the surface. The crew were later persuaded to come back aboard and sailed their ship away from the noise that they had all thought was a ticking time fuze inside a mine.

Before long, another officer, Lieutenant Hood – a brave man who detested diving but was still determined to work with us – joined our party to replace Lieutenant Bailey. On his very first dive, while he was diving with me, he went down the port side of a heavily loaded merchant vessel and I the starboard. Finding nothing my side, I surfaced alongside the rudder as was normal, signalled that all was clear and climbed into the diving launch that was waiting at the stern. We anxiously waited for my 'buddy' diver to surface but sadly he did not. Lieutenant Commander Crabb and I plunged into the sea and searched the ship's bottom and around the area for a long time but to no avail. Lieutenant Hood's body was not recovered for many days but was eventually found floating at the western end of the runway by an RAF sentry. Lieutenant Hood had dragged his goggles and breathing gear down round his neck in his last struggles for breath and had also torn off one of his weighted gym shoes. We presumed that he may have had oxygen poisoning or the weight of his gym shoes had dragged him to his death, but we later found that this very brave man suffered from bronchial attacks but even that did not stop him from volunteering to dive and search for mines. This incident only goes to show the very real danger we encountered day by day and his death affected us all profoundly, as he was our first fatality.

We hoped that our party could have buried our brave companion at sea out in the bay with the honour he deserved but for some unknown reason this was carried out by a Royal Navy ship on its way to Oran in North Africa.

On many occasions I found that our D.S.E.A breathing apparatus was inadequate for our work, especially the amount of oxygen that the very small bottle carried which, under strenuous working conditions, would last no more than 15 to 20 minutes, after which, without warning, we often got no oxygen when demanded. This resulted in a tearing off of our weighted shoes and a strenuous dash to the surface, again for a change of oxygen bottle or breathing set.

When Italy entered the war, an innocent-looking merchant ship named the *Olterra* limped out of the Mediterranean and into the Spanish port of Algeciras, only a few miles across the bay from Gibraltar; her engine was supposedly broken down. In the autumn of 1942, Italian naval officers and engineers arrived secretly in Algeciras and started work turning the *Olterra* into an Italian Trojan Horse – a base for two-man torpedo attacks on Gibraltar. The Spanish were led to believe that the ship was simply having repairs but this was not the case; they were busy cutting a large door into the hull, just below the water line, for the exit and entry of the two-man torpedoes that were to be assembled inside her hull.

The Olterra, showing secret hatch (normally below waterline).

This idea came from an engineer and clever technician, Antonio Ramogino, who had been detailed to investigate the area between Gibraltar and the nearby Spanish coast in order to establish a secret base from where the Gruppa Gamma frogmen could attack the Allied shipping at anchor. He found a perfect answer in the Villa Carmela, on the north coast of the bay very near to La Linea, which he rented with his Spanish wife – the charming Senora Conchita (who I was to meet later in Venice, when she referred to the villa as the most advanced base of the Italian Navy in enemy waters). They occupied the villa on the pretence of being on an extended honeymoon.

This base was ideal for the Tenth Flotilla, who could continue attacking while waiting for the Two Man Torpedoes to be completed. One of the Italian frogmen, Petty Officer Vago Giari, was to become a very good friend and diving buddy of mine and Lieutenant Commander Crabb's during our activities in Italy a few years later. Vago told me that the position of the Villa Carmela was a dream come true. Torpedoes and breathing apparatus, under many disguises, were smuggled into Spain from Italy under Foreign Office seal and it was from the *Olterra* that, when the divers of the Tenth Flotilla Mass and the Gruppa Gamma arrived from Italy in 1942, operations started in Gibraltar.

Diver Vago Giari of the Italian Gruppa Gamma.

One night, led by Lieutenant Commander Notari, three two-man torpedoes, which the Italians called pigs (*maiales*), passed through Olterra's underwater door. The attack was very successful; they sank the 4,875-ton *Camerata*, badly damaged the 7,000-ton American Liberty ship *Pat Harrison* and also damaged the 7,500-ton *Mahsud*, after which, all three two-man torpedo crews returned safely to base.

A similar attack, but from the Italian submarine *Scire*, had been made in December 1941 by Lieutenant de La Penna and PO Bianchi on the Royal Navy battle ships *Valiant* and *Queen Elizabeth* in Alexandria harbour, Egypt. Both ships sank, but sat on the bottom in shallow water. This action, and the Italians' extraordinary courage in riding their two-man torpedoes, had swung the balance of sea power in the Mediterranean.

Many attacks were made on shipping in the anchorage of Gibraltar, both from the *Olterra* and the Villa Carmela, which was close to the shore in La Linea and only 400 yards from a convoy of merchant ships anchored there.

Of course, all the details of these operations only came to light after Italy had capitulated.

At the time, I and the other divers discarded a popular theory that the enemy frogmen were dropped by parachute. In Jumper's Bastion, "Rattler" Morgan strongly upheld a view (which Lieutenant Crabb had unintentionally passed on to him) that the enemy came from the *Olterra*. It stood to reason, Morgan argued. He hinted that he had also heard something from the crew of the daily water boat, which backed his suspicions – namely, that the Italian tanker was not lying there for nothing. I strongly agreed.

By this time, Crabb had been promoted to Lieutenant-Commander and had been awarded the George Medal and was very overworked. We wanted to help him, so, unbeknown to anyone, Morgan and I decided to investigate the rumours. Each day from Algeciras the small Spanish water tanker *Blossom* came across to Gibraltar to top up the Rock's drinking water supply, and twice every day she was searched by us for mines. On her regular passage to the Rock, the water tanker had to pass through lines of anchored Allied shipping, making them a very good target. (Before the Italian Gruppa Gamma frogmen arrived in Spain, the German officer Frederick Hummel of the Kampfschwimmers had bribed the crew of *Blossom* to give him passage into these rows of allied ships, whereupon he very bravely tried to lay mines under the ships, wearing only Drager ex U-Boat escape breathing apparatus, but failed.)

We became very friendly with the tanker crew and, after protracted and secret negotiations with them, plus several bottles of whisky, they agreed to take us across the bay to Algeciras. For this journey we dressed as Spanish boatmen and were tipped off by the water boat crew when to slip ashore. We made no mention that we were going on a spying trip, of course. Our declared reason for entering Spain was that we had served on the Rock for two years and had not enjoyed the company of a woman in all that time (true) and that we intended to visit a Brothel.

The *Olterra* was moored at the end of the seaward mole, almost an hour's sweltering walk from the area where we had landed. There was a Spanish sentry on the gangway but I just tossed him a loud Spanish greeting of *hola* as we casually walked by, to which he answered with a lazy grunt. A number of obviously Italian naval ratings were lounging on her deck, their disguise very poor – a mixture of civilian and naval uniforms – and there were far more of them than would have been required for an interned ship.

We went to a café way out on the exterior mole but in sight of the *Olterra*; the great bulk of the Rock towered up behind her across the bay, and together "Rattler" and I shook hands, for we had at last proved that the Italian ship was a "Trojan Horse". The café atmosphere was heady with conspiracy. All around us we heard conversations in German and other languages. Spain was full of spies and I am sure that the Spanish regime under General Franco was well aware of this. In the end, we left the café for we had to return to the water boat in order to be back in Gibraltar before dusk. We had hidden our uniforms in a shed on the dockside in Gibraltar and heading back had a shock when we were stopped by two British military policemen who menacingly said in English "Curfew. It's gone 11 o'clock". "*No entendido*,"

I replied, to which he said to his companion, "Maybe they are on night work – *trabajo noche*?"

"*Si, si,*" I replied, and they both smiled, turned around and walked away, leaving us with thumping hearts as we dressed and then made our way to our mess in Jumper's Bastion. As we swung into our hammocks, we drew little attention except from the Commander's parrot, mocking us as usual!

"Good Night Baron," said Rattler but I found it very difficult to sleep, for my mind was whirling with thoughts. What had happened to my life? I could have pinched myself! I was just a young man with a poor education who had joined the Royal Navy as a second-class stoker only a couple of years before ... and now, here I was, spying for my country in a foreign land... It was a very restless night.

The following day, Morgan and I, with much trepidation and expecting to be in the cells by nightfall, informed Lieutenant-Commander Crabb of our exploits. His first reaction was to literally 'bristle' as he growled, "Good God, Knowles!" and then, chuckling loudly. "This is proof of my suspicions ... and with regard to you two, this is as far as it goes." He laughed. "Now get out of here!" I shook hands with Rattler and sighed with relief, for we both sensed that he was very satisfied with our report.

But that was not the end of it, for when CPO Thorpe heard of our escapade he gave us a tremendous bollocking and stamped off in a furious rage, but later, as I walked past him he gave me a little grin and a wink. A couple of days later, when in the company of Commander Hancock, he stared at me. I expected him to speak but he just lowered his eyebrows, pursed his lips and shook his head from side to side.

Our suspicions regarding the *Olterra* having proved correct, our party discussed the possibility of reversing the situation, and came up with many wild ideas of returning some of the mines they had placed on our ships and putting her out of action. This idea went higher up the chain of command as far as the Admiralty but was flatly refused, much to our disappointment. We were powerless to do anything about it, as the ship was lying in the waters of neutral Spain and any action of this type could have resulted in a backlash from General Franco.[9]

One night a sentry in Gibraltar spotted a disturbance in the water, just off the Detached Mole, and suddenly a two-man torpedo from the *Olterra* burst to the surface, due to a steering fault, and the Italian divers Manisco and Varini were spotted and captured. The Commander and I were fortunately nearby and took our first "war trophies" – a pair of swim-fins each! The same night, another torpedo was spotted and sunk by a depth charge, killing Lieutenant Visintini and PO Magro. Their bodies were recovered some days later and brought ashore.

During this night attack, all the other British divers were busy groping under the Allied ships in the darkness for mines or charges, dragging themselves along the keels as usual but my boss and I swam like frogs underwater, using our captured fins. Nothing was found but for the Italians it had been a very expensive night.

Commander Crabb inquired about arrangements for the burial of our enemies – the bodies were still in the mortuary – and learnt that their disposal was a matter for the maintenance department. Our group thought this very callous. Some days later, all the members of our diving group boarded the diving launch and sailed out into the bay with the Italian dead, their bodies draped under Italian flags. We saluted them and committed these very brave men to the deep from whence they had come. Our gesture was little understood at the time by other services on the Rock but in Italy a year later we discovered that our action of burying the dead with great respect had been observed by the Italian Frogmen in the Villa Carmella only about 400 metres away.

[9] In the 1950s, after Commander Crabb disappeared, a film was made about our exploit, entitled *The Silent Enemy* but the directors replaced 'Rattler' Morgan with Commander Crabb – no doubt to attract more interest in the film – and some of the actions in the film did not take place at all.

Our war was a chivalrous one and we had great respect for our enemy – and, as I found out later, they had equal respect for us.

Both the Italian Tenth Light Flotilla divers and ourselves, the Underwater Working Party (how I hated that title in the beginning) were young, athletic, friendly and carefree but, above all, we were intensely human and loved life.

On 4th July 1943 our team was working out at Europa Point, searching for mines under the merchant ships at anchor, when we heard the roar of engines from an aircraft taking off. But the noise ceased abruptly and the plane crashed into the sea. We, of course, leapt into our launch and roared towards the accident, hoping to render assistance, but the plane had sunk just off the Eastern end of the runway, a good distance from where we were, and only one survivor was found, the pilot, who was floating on the surface. We dived, hoping to find more survivors, but in vain.

The following day we were informed that the plane was carrying General Sikorski, Commander-in-Chief of the Polish Armed Forces and Prime Minister of the Polish Government in Exile from 1940-43. We dived to search for the body of the general, who had in his possession very important secret documents, relating, I believe, to the Second Front.

We found the plane lying on its back. There appeared to be very little structural damage, except for an area on the port side and just astern of the wing, which had been torn open, and this allowed us entry. Over time we retrieved 16 bodies and documents.

Visibility inside the plane was very difficult, due to the fact that it had been carrying many cases of cigarettes and cigars, which had burst open on impact and badly stained the water. We also came across cases of brandy, whisky, etc, and many rolls of silk. During my search inside the aircraft I recall seeing a small packing case with a badly-stained address label reading either Ribbens or Rueben's Hotel London. I don't know what it contained or if it ever got to its destination, but for some unknown reason this address has remained in my mind over the years.

We, The Underwater Working Party – I am now very proud of our title – continued diving for several days in and around the area where the plane crashed, to retrieve any remaining articles or documents, but mysteriously we were unable to find the body of Sofia Lesinowska, the General's daughter. She was never found and I doubted that she was ever aboard.

The body of General Sikorski was taken to England onboard the Polish destroyer *Orkan* and buried in Newark cemetery. In 1993 his remains were disinterred and flown to Warsaw, where they now lie in Wawel cathedral. There was speculation that General Sikorski's plane – a Polish Air Transport Command aircraft that had brought him from Cairo to Gibraltar – had been sabotaged, as it was declared defective and unsafe prior to his departure from Gibraltar. As a result, the following day Sikorski had taken off in another plane (the one we were now searching), a converted Liberator Bomber AL-523, staffed by British aircrew. Twenty-four hours later, Sikorski's original plane left Gibraltar, still with its own Polish aircrew, and arrived safely in England.

The cause of the incident and crash remains a mystery to this day, for no hard evidence has come to light, but there have been many theories. It is strongly believed that the plane was sabotaged but this was never properly investigated and no comment ever came from the British Government, although I feel they had a hand in it (in fact, in my estimation, an arm).

It is now known that Sir Peter Chalmers Mitchell, an intellectual and a Communist, lived in Malaga and was in touch with the traitors Philby, Burgess and McLean during the war. One strong theory is that Stalin, who later took Poland, wanted Sikorski out of the way.

In Gibraltar, a plaque in Devils Tower road and a memorial commemorate the event. A list of the bodies we recovered is as follows:

General Sikorski – Polish C-in-C and President-in-exile
Col Izycki (Head of Polish aircrew)
Gen Klimecki
Col Javecki
Jan Gralewski
Lt Ponikiewski
Adam Kulakowski
Lt Col Victor Cazelet (MP)
Brigadier J P Whitely (MP)
And the British aircrew (names unknown)

It has been reported by various authors in books about the Sikorski incident that the plane was searched first by 'local divers'. This is not true, however, for the only diving apparatus available in 1943 was DSEA, the gear that our party the UWWP used. Another frequent claim is that the plane was searched by Crabb and Bill Bailey, but this is clearly a mistake because Lieutenant Bailey had departed from the UWWP many months previously and returned to the UK with a broken ankle. Another author even reports that Lord Victor Rothschild was visiting Gibraltar at the time of the crash and interviewed Crabb and Bailey at the scene, but this was impossible for, as I have stated, Bailey had left many months before and my mind is very clear on that issue, for he was often my Buddy diver.

The only other member of our party who was not present at the crash scene was Chief Petty Officer Ralph Thorpe, who was having ear trouble after a previous dive and was visiting the military hospital and therefore unable to assist us in our search of the crashed plane.

Another plane was to crash in the bay; an Albacore crewed by RAF personnel, with the loss of all the crew. Although we dashed over in our diving launch, we were unable to save anyone and found ourselves swimming in almost pure petrol on the surface, for the plane had broken its wing and the fuel tank had burst.

The very same day I nearly lost my own life when a giant cable-laying ship was leaving her mooring near to the pen where our diving launch lay. I was aboard at the time, checking the engine, when I heard a grinding noise and suddenly the launch was lifted violently beneath me, tearing the vessel into two pieces and ultimately throwing me into the water and then sucking me below the surface before washing me in a powerful wake along the dock-side wall, closely followed by the wreck of what remained of our vessel. It seems the ship had too much way on her, and before either her engines or her back springs could pull her up, she had crushed our diving launch. The incident was reported by CPO Thorpe, who was a witness, and described the scene as follows: "The launch was crushed like a biscuit in the hand and 'Baron' Knowles popped up between the fingers."

This incident left us without a dive boat, so Lieutenant-Commander Crabb asked the RAF for the loan of a Tender to take its place. This highlights how very poorly equipped we were for our very important and dangerous work. For instance, our base in Jumpers Bastion was situated just below the Alameda Gardens (where today the lift station is situated that takes tourists to the top of the Rock) and this was a long way from our action station when an emergency arose and we had to get to our Tender on the North Mole. Our only form of transport was three butcher's bikes! With our diving gear carried in the large wicker baskets on the front, we sped down Main Street with bells ringing, through the gates at Casemates square and along North Mole to our Tender.

In Gibraltar during the war there was an 11pm curfew and the streets were deserted except for the Military Police, who were instructed to give us free passage without delay. The Commander was a very good cyclist and when a flap occurred he would offer an extra tot of rum to any man who could race him to the Tender.

Just after his promotion the Lieutenant-Commander left Jumpers Bastion and moved with other senior officers into the Rock Hotel, situated half way up the rock.

The mention of rum reminds me of the day we were visited by Admiral Sir Frederick Edward-Collins, the temporary Governor of Gibraltar, who arrived in his beautiful big launch, which we would have given our hind teeth for. He was very impressed with our work and asked "Tell me Crabb, do you get any extra pay for this type of work?" He was informed that we were paid 'danger money', the extra pay being fixed at 9d a day for a rating, 1s 3d for a petty officer and 1s 6d for an officer. Sir Frederick declared that this was nonsense considering the very dangerous work we were engaged in and that all ranks should be paid an extra half-crown.

"Now what more can I get you?" Sir Frederick asked, and the Commander replied, "The water is very cold, Sir. May I suggest extra rum?" I remember getting the rum, but never the extra money placed upon the top of my proffered cap on pay day (we never had paypackets).

On many long night dives the water was so piercingly cold that by morning we found ourselves well under the influence, having downed many tots in our efforts to keep warm and to slow down the violent shivering of our bodies. I was to discover that although we at times became rather drunk, we never suffered from hangovers and we put this down to the amount of pure oxygen we were breathing, which seemed to counteract the normal effect of the alcohol.

By now the amount of shipping in the anchorage of Gibraltar was so huge that it became impossible for our small party, which was starved of reasonable equipment, to search the bottom of every ship. False alarms rang with ferocious regularity – even the slightest splash or bubbles in the water would result in a sentry calling 'action stations' and once again it was onto our butcher's bikes and a rapid swoop down Main Street, at any hour, night or day. All ships' captains had been instructed to rig bottom lines that could be dragged from bow to stern by their own crew to feel for possible obstructions and to enable the divers rapid entry, but on one ship we boarded there was not even a watch-keeper and we walked along the deck, unchallenged, all the way to the master's cabin. This resulted in Commander Crabb furiously raving at the Captain and Mate.

On our rare nights off, PO David "Dinger" Bell and I took a drink in our favourite bar, the Trocadero in Main St, where we would meet other sailors and troops, all wearing shorts for the first time and very obvious with their white knees. They were on the way to Malta and North Africa from ships passing through. On discovering that we were based on the Rock, they were of the impression that we had a cushy number. We had no reason to enlighten them as to the true nature of our job!

Life on the Rock of Gibraltar was far from normal. Except for a few female nurses there were no women or children; all of them having been evacuated to England or the West Indies at the outbreak of war.

The RAF Squadron Leader who loaned us our diving tender was keen to experience a dive and asked if I would teach him. To oblige him, I took him underwater a couple of times and this led to him inviting me on a flight from the Rock out into the Med in a two-seater fighter – a Defiant Mk.II. This was the very first flight of my life and I found it thrilling. I was sitting between two guns and he said, "If you see any enemy aircraft and I shout 'FIRE,' line them up and press the red buttons." I don't recall him instructing me to release the safety catches, so I must presume it was a joke.

Without any notice and upon the eve of what was potentially one of the most devastating attacks ever, the Tenth Flotilla and the Gruppa Gamma heard on the radio that Italy had negotiated an immediate Armistice with the Allies. The situation had now changed and apart from a few absolute Fascist officers plus their Commander Prince Borghese, who decided to fight on, the majority of the Italian divers hated the Nazis and also the fact that they would no longer be supported by the Germans, who still occupied a large proportion of their country. At a meeting of the units and after much discussion they decided to get through the German lines and head south, to join up with the American 5th Army. Many simply went home to their families.

One of the Italian divers was later to become my very good friend and buddy diver. Vago Giari told me that when Italy capitulated he was in Venice at the HQ of the Tenth Flotilla, training and preparing for an attack on New York, and that this operation was in an advanced stage of preparation and had been fixed to take place in December. However, his priorities changed when he heard that the German attitude towards the Italian civilian population had altered and that they were committing many atrocities against men, women and children of their former Allies. He told me that at one period of attempting to get through the German lines he had to undress a dead soldier and use his uniform to help with his progress. His home was in the port of Livorno (Leghorn) which was still in the hands of the Germans. On arriving home he discovered that his wife Liliana had been injured while trying to oppose looting troops; this led to him becoming a very valuable member of the UWWP and a lifelong friend and diving companion.

As time wore on the attacks by the enemy Italian frogmen on Gibraltar diminished, although we were obliged to continue our routine of diving every dawn on any ships in the harbour. Finally, in September 1943, Italy capitulated and the Admiralty presumed that Gibraltar was no longer under threat from them. The Royal Navy Underwater Working Party disbanded and all its members headed back to UK for a well-earned leave – all, that is, except Lieutenant-Commander Crabb and me, for I had volunteered to accompany him on a roving mission to Italy and France.

Until Michael Jung, the director of the Hans-Hass-Institute of Submarine Research and Diving Technology and author of the book *Agenten unter Wasser* sent me a copy of his book, I had not the slightest idea that Germany was ever involved in attacks on Gibraltar. Although I was aware of their very successful attack on the bridge at Nijmegen, they had never before claimed any success on the Rock.

In order to increase military collaboration with their German allies, the Italian Tenth Flotilla had decided to pass on their vast knowledge of underwater warfare to them and a number of German swimmer pupils, under the command of Lieutenant-Commander von Martiny, attended training courses in the port of Leghorn (Livorno), all under the command of Lieutenant Wolk, the very tough Italian instructor and ex-Olympic swimmer. This included the Italians supplying breathing gear, rubber suits, fins, etc. It is obvious that German intelligence had no knowledge that we, the Underwater Working Party, had wound up our activities and left the Rock, for there was still a tremendous amount of Allied merchant shipping in the port and bay, on the way to Italy to supply the American 5th and Allied 8th Armies. I am sure that if the new German underwater attack group had been aware of this, there would have been a new and devastating offensive on Gibraltar.

4. To Italy and France

In May 1944 Lieutenant-Commander Crabb and I left Gibraltar aboard a Royal Navy landing craft bound for Naples Italy, where we found the volcano Vesuvius erupting and ash falling all over the city. The crash and rumble of collapsing buildings could be heard, as the seething rivers of red hot lava tore away anything in their path. After many days and a trip to the Allied HQ in Caserta, we scrounged an American 6x6 lorry (covered in volcanic ash) and, after cleaning the air intake and filter, I managed to get the engine running and returned to Naples, loaded up our diving gear, six foot long bottles of oxygen to top up the small bottles of our diving sets, then loaded the RMS (render mines safe) anti-magnetic tools and food (i.e. tins of corned beef and cases of American 'C rations', plus many very heavy Jerry cans of drinking water)then, with a roving commission, headed north towards Rome on the only open road.

I found that when driving an American 6x6 lorry I would meet hundreds of similar vehicles and the practise was to salute each other as we passed by switching the ignition off and on and causing a backfire. Most of them were driven by American Negro soldiers, members of the famous 92nd Red Bull Express Division that in WW2 distinguished itself delivering ammunition and supplies, often in very dangerous and terrible conditions, on Highway 6 up the Liri Valley and in every battlefield of the war.

The job given to us was to clear mines and bombs from any ports on the west coast that the American 5th Army could use to land supplies. Our very first port was Chivitavechia, but before we could start our underwater searches, an American intelligence group informed us that there had been no enemy activity in the harbour. It was only later that we found this information to be incorrect. That night I slept in a cell at the town's deserted prison and woke up smothered in fleas. I took myself off to the harbour, strapped on a breathing set and, fully clothed (including boots) plunged from the jetty into the water, where I sat for 20 minutes on the seabed in about five fathoms. This removed the creatures but unfortunately not their bites!

We left Chivitavechia and headed north and came across what remained of Monte Cassino and saw the red and white Polish flag still flying proudly above the ruin of the once great monastery, where they had recently fought so bravely and left so many hundreds of dead behind. There was little left to see after the terrible pounding of the bombing – some 578 tons onto the monastery and over 1,000 tons onto the little town of Cassino at the foot of the mountain – plus hours and hours of artillery fire from the joint allied attack that it had required to remove the Germans from this defensive position, the monastery finally being taken in a joint attack comprising Polish, Indian and New Zealand troops. The road was now open for the Allied troops to advance to Rome but a great price had been paid, as anyone today visiting this battleground can see in the numerous cemeteries, containing lines and lines of hundreds of military graves.

Behind this vast burial area on the side of the road we came across the remains of a farmhouse that had been badly damaged in the bombing raids and through the open barn doors I spotted a civilian Italian lorry, covered with a badly holed tarpaulin sheet, which I rescued and cut into two body-length groundsheets for my boss and me, for I anticipated many rough times ahead for us both.

In Rome, which had just been liberated, we joined up with an American intelligence group at the Hotel Nationalli. The entire front area was protected by a large semi-circle of sandbags and barbed wire, making the building a very safe HQ from any attacks. The group was commanded by Lieutenant-Commander Tony Marsloe, ex Assistant District Attorney of New York, who informed us that the day after we left Civitavechia a small Royal Navy vessel with a crew of 19 had been blown up as it entered the port at night and there were no survivors. She was a converted wooden trawler used for minesweeping and had made contact with a drifting horned or pressure mine as she entered the port in darkness. This increased our determination to judge for ourselves whether or not a port was clear and not rely on local intelligence. This hotel afforded me the last opportunity to sleep in a real bed for many months to come.

Commander Crabb, a devout Catholic, organised a visit to St Peters Basilica and invited me to accompany him. We were probably the first persons to enter after the liberation. I remember little of what should have been a very memorable occasion, except entering a cavernous, empty place, accompanied by a little Irish priest, his voice echoing as he pointed out areas of special interest. During our visit, the priest knelt to pray at the entrance to a small chapel and my boss joined him. I was invited to join them but I refused and walked away. I had lost my faith during the many awful times I had gone through on the Malta Convoys and the numerous horrific sounds and scenes of death I had experienced. I was, at that time, angry with God and did not want to speak to him. It would be another twenty years before I again visited the Basilica, then to be only one of millions. Commander Crabb always referred to Catholic Priests as 'God's Butlers'.

We left Rome and headed north and at one time found ourselves leading an armoured brigade towards Florence. We were ripped off by an angry American high-ranking officer, who was amazed at my 6x6 lorry flying the Royal Navy White Ensign and demanded to know "What the bloody hell is the Limey navy doing here?" We had earlier been very near to death when, on emerging from a wooded area and creating a great cloud of dust, we came within 200 yards of a Tiger Tank of the 14th Panzer, which fired at us, fortunately missing us but bringing down a very large branch of a tree above, that came crashing down onto the cab and smashed our windscreen.

Lieutenant Douglas, a land mine disposal officer who was accompanying us, suffered a severe cut to his forehead. Before I had clearly grasped the situation, Commander Crabb, who was driving, had our vehicle in reverse and going like a rocket back into the woods. I don't know who was the more surprised, the German Tiger Tank crew or us. Members of the Army Medical Corps were soon in attendance and rushed Lieutenant Douglas away for treatment. It was some time before he could return to duty.

We later forded the river Arno and entered Florence, under very heavy German sniping and shelling.

Our very first job was to get two important military persons and members of the American OSS to a meeting with a group of partisans at a very battered HQ at the corner of the Via Porta Rossa, close to the Ponte Veccio, on the north side of the river. This was to be done in the dead of night but one of them declined when he saw what the crossing would involve. The three of us set off, part-stumbling and part swimming across, with the OSS officer between us. He never uttered a word during our passage but gave out plenty grunts and groans, although I don't know why, because the water was lovely and warm. One loud protestation from him invited a long burst of machine gun tracer fire, which slapped into the water just ahead of us. I could see them coming towards me at great speed, as I hoped I would not be hit, but noticed how slow they appeared when passing and dying away into the distance.

We were kept under heavy fire for most of the night during our attempt to return to the south bank over what remained of the Ponte Santa Trinita bridge, which took an amazing number of bullets in the enemy's attempt to dislodge us. I can still hear, to this day, the very distinctive scream of ricochets as they struck the stone buttress we crouched behind until dawn when the firing died down and it was safer to scramble back. We were both wearing our fins and it proved very difficult to scramble over the rocks in the shallow parts of the river but we did not remove them, for they had become very precious to us. We then came under fire from our destination, where an American machine gun post had spotted us and opened fire. We both dived head first into a deep pool that lay ahead of us, then cautiously lifted our heads. A few minutes later we heard a voice shouting orders to cease fire. This was the second time that Yank 'intelligence' had let us down and we came to the conclusion that the GIs were all trigger-happy. As we crawled onto the south buttress of the Ponte Vecchio bridge further downstream my boss turned to me and said "Bloody Hell, Knowles!"

"Yes Sir," I replied. "Bloody Hell!"

Three days later we were able to drive across the river on a hastily erected Bailey bridge. We found wonderful billets in the abandoned Excelsior Hotel, but we did not sleep well that night, nor for the next week, due to the heavy shelling day and night and the constant street fighting.

On discovering that we were divers, a crazy Florentine assumed we had been sent to recover statues that had been blown into the Arno and implored us to be very, very careful with them. I shook my head in disbelief and wondered if I would ever emerge from this lunacy with a normal mind.

My most harrowing job in Florence was to remove a putrefying corpse that was lying exposed on the debris of the Ponte Santa Trinita Bridge. I swam out into the river and drifted down onto the heaps of massive stones that were all that remained of the great structure. The stench from the corpse was horrific and I was glad I was breathing oxygen from my DSEA re-Breather apparatus and not from the air around me. I was amazed at the number of people, mostly American troops and a few civilians, who were watching me from the riverbanks and the nearby ancient Ponte Veccio bridge further downstream of me, all of them pinching their noses or covering their faces with a handkerchief or a khaki scarf in an attempt to blank out the stench of putrefaction.

On my return to our HQ I was aware that I had brought back the awful smell of the corpse with me, for everyone was giving me a wide berth. I took at least half a dozen cold showers, for there was no hot water available and, with the use of a large block of carbolic soap given to me by the hotel cleaner, I finally cleansed myself of the terrible stench of death.

One day I drove into the north of the city, hoping to find a group of English or Allied soldiers who could supply my boss and I with food, and more importantly drink, for our Jerry Cans were empty. Although there was plenty of water available locally, it was not fit to drink.

I was arrested by an American Military Police patrol, who could not understand what or who I was – a strangely-dressed man, carrying an American intelligence pass, stating that he was a diver, speaking with a Lancashire accent, wearing a British khaki uniform, carrying a .38 revolver on each thigh and wearing an American helmet, from under which was peeping a red woollen diver's bonnet. I was also driving a Yankee 6x6 lorry containing many boxes of American C Rations (which, by then, was our only food and all I was able to scrounge). After a few hours I was released without an apology, but followed by the comment "Crazy Limey!" and returned to the hotel and our HQ.

I enjoyed working amongst the Americans, they were different. One thing that dawned on me was that they were quiet, that is, there was no crashing of steel-studded boots that the British army wore, for the boots of the Yanks were rubber-soled and fairly silent. Also, although they had only just arrived from America, many of them sported lines of medal ribbons. One of the Military Police, a sergeant, showed me a Purple Heart that had been awarded to him after he was hit by ricochet high on the shoulder. This, he stated, had taken place on the practice rifle range back in the States. We compared our war wounds and I must admit that his medal looked better than my injury certificate, but who was the prouder?

The main reason for our visit to Florence, so far from the sea, was because we had received information that the Two Man Torpedo and all the diving gear for the Tenth Flotilla

MAS were assembled there. We did find this factory, in fact, and a great amount of stores, but unfortunately no diving suits were found.

One afternoon, accompanied by Lieutenant-Commander Marsloe, the American leader of the intelligence group, we were driving towards the factory when our 6x6 lorry came under fire, for sporadic violence was still going on. We were attacked from both sides from the roofs of buildings on the Porta Romano, with many of the bullets striking the tram-lines in front of us and ricochets hitting our windshield, showering us with glass. This was followed by German stick grenades. I changed gear quickly and rapidly sped out of the range of the explosions. We were soon joined by troops from the Light Horse, a South African Kimberly Regiment and tanks of the B Squadron Special Service Battalion who, although under heavy fire and sniping, managed to kill many of the attackers and soon drove the enemy back.

On another occasion Lieutenant Commander Marsloe, the American intelligence group leader, contacted us again to inform us that his American intelligence group were holding a young Italian officer who claimed that he was a former member of the Italian Tenth Flotilla. Marsloe, being of Italian decent and having a fluent command of the language, had spoken with the young man, who had told him that he was Sub-Lieutenant Ventorini and he wished to supply us with information about the present and continuing operations of Prince Borghese and the remaining members of the Gruppa Gamma divers, who were still loyal to Mussolini and operating from La Spezia. Also, he had very important information regarding a new type of limpet mine that was impossible to remove without it exploding, on which the time clock was usually set to detonate either thirty-six or forty-eight hours after being fitted to the bilge keel of a ship. However, this information was not new to the Underwater Working Party, for we had dealt with this type of mine in Gibraltar a year before. This was the mine that we dared not move until we had burnt off the area of the bilge keel it was attached to. Ventorini also stated that the Tenth Flotilla would attack ships at anchor in the invaded ports of North West Italy and we had to get this information urgently to Allied HQ in Caserta.

Ventorini was a dark and slender young man, aged about twenty years and was immaculately dressed in shirt and shorts, wearing the flashes of a Partisan brigade. He was to remain with Commander Crabb and me to serve in whatever capacity my boss thought fit.

Our next operation was to clear from underwater any mines and bombs in the port of Livorno (Leghorn), only a few miles south of La Spezia, which was still the HQ of the Italian frogmen and two-man torpedo operators, under the command of Prince Borghese, and they were still a very great danger to allied shipping, which, after we had cleared the port, would now be very much nearer to them.

The Commander and I parted from the American ICU (Intelligence Collecting Unit) and prepared ourselves for a repeat of Gibraltar, for we knew that when Allied shipping entered Leghorn harbour the Italian frogmen in La Spezia still faithful to Mussolini would attack. Vicious fighting was also still going on between the American 5th Army and the Germans.

Keeping just behind the front line, we headed south to the beautiful walled city of Sienna, famous for its furious horse races around the main square and the nearest point from which we could get to the coast and on to our objective. It was becoming a very fluid war and villages were changing hands with extraordinary rapidity.

With no desire to get ahead again and lead the American 5th Army into battle, so we ended up camped out in an olive grove for a few days, where I spent much of my time looking for eggs, rabbits, chickens or anything to supplement our meagre rations. Barbarism was evident everywhere and during these searches I would often come upon the naked, decomposing bodies of dead Germans who had been stripped of all their possessions by the Italian partisans, but never buried. In these areas the stench of death was horrific. Also, in the orchards I had to be very, very careful of booby-traps, especially Butterfly Bombs that hung from trees and bushes and shoe-mines hidden in the grass. Many of these devices had trip-wires attached to them and walking through an olive grove I must have looked like a ballet dancer crossing a stage while avoiding many box mines, for I had become very expert at spotting them.

Finding food was no easy task, as the retreating Germans had laid this area of Tuscany bare, but although the villagers were themselves near to starvation I was still offered a small Pullet egg or a little bread here and there. In our makeshift camp my bed was a strip of tarpaulin lying on the ground under the lorry while Commander Crabb, being an officer, had the privilege of sleeping in the vehicle itself. I found it amazing that at ground level I was never bothered by mosquitoes, yet only about six feet higher my companion had a hell of a night. But I could never persuade him to crawl under the vehicle, where I had prepared groundsheets from the tarpaulin I had liberated for us.

We eventually received news that Leghorn had fallen to a partisan attack and that they were holding the port and would allow us entry for inspection. However, because the allied front line lay several miles to the south, the only possible way of reaching our objective was by sea. Due to the importance of our task, we were provided with a Royal Navy Motor Gun Boat and crew, which resulted in a hair-raising 40-knot dash north up the coast, during which we were shelled every mile of the way by Howitzer coastal guns that had a range of many miles. The German gunnery was amazing, for although we were a number of miles from the coast, we had often to take evasive action as a shell would burst into the sea just ahead of our speeding boat and we were constantly drenched by great columns of water that shot up. The snow-white wash of our speeding craft as we sped into a northerly and oncoming sea was making us an excellent target and this continued until we got closer inshore and the

German Howitzers, I presumed, could not aim their barrels any lower.

Some time later my boss informed me that German intelligence had been well aware of our operations and had tried to put us out of action. At that time, he told me, we were at the top of the German 'hit list' in Italy.

At last we arrived near a small beach and swam and floated ourselves and our gear ashore. Again, we were thankful to our captured Italian swim fins, which assisted us in a number of laborious swims through very high surf to the beach near the Leghorn harbour breakwater. Then, making our farewells and thanking the crew of the MGB, we dragged ourselves and our gear ashore.

We were greeted on the beach near the breakwater by a large group of vicious-looking partisans, both men and women, all wearing red communist scarves around their necks. They also had, under guard, a group of German prisoners, who shouted at us in loud protesting voices and pointed to a couple of their dead companions lying in a mined area nearby.

"Have you got the message Knowles?" My boss commented. "We are in a bloody awful situation."

"These look a bloody rough gang," I said.

"Yes, and don't stare at their women," he replied.

Sensing we were in a volatile situation we felt very ill at ease and continually watched our backs and the weapons we carried.

The German prisoners pointed again at the mangled bodies of their two dead comrades and continued to protest loudly. It looked suspiciously as though the Germans had been forcibly made to walk into a mined area, for a number of warning signs declaring ACHTUNG MINEN could be plainly seen.

We camped with the partisans for several uncomfortable days and nights. The nights were very noisy and it was almost dawn before the drinking, dancing and singing ceased. They were an unruly mob and not typical of the many brave and disciplined groups that existed in Italy, who fought tooth and nail against their former allies the Germans. We were not allowed to advance until the partisans had completed looting the port area to their satisfaction and only then did they provide us with a small, chain-driven German Opel utility vehicle.

After loading our bergens with diving gear, anti-magnetic tools, gag, bronze spanner, motor horn, etc, we finally departed, drove into the port and got down to the business of searching underwater for mines or other obstructions. Again wearing our captured Italian fins, we found the work beneath the surface much simpler and were thankful that the heavy gym shoes would no longer be required.

We laid down a rough grid and started our underwater search with much trepidation, for the Germans had started shelling the port with a short range artillery barrage and the stinging, stinking smell of cordite drifted over the port. During our diving, shells constantly exploded on and under the surface. Underwater these explosions sounded horrific and very, very near to us. After a while we became concussed and found it very painful as they hit the surface of the water around us and sent out great waves of pressure. After one nearby explosion I felt that my eyeballs were about to pop out. We swam to the surface to find that, in fact, we were safer remaining underwater because of the amount of shrapnel that was flying through the air, although from time to time we had to climb onto the jetty in order to change our oxygen bottles. This we did in the shelter of the lighthouse, with one eye on the incoming shells. While taking shelter on one such occasion we saw our little German Opel wagon, which was parked on an adjoining jetty, take a number of heavy shrapnel direct hits and we were afraid that our diving gear, plus all the tackle we needed to render mines safe, may go up in smoke.

This was a more hazardous situation than Gibraltar and we both sighed with relief when the shelling ceased. The following day both the Commander and I complained of various aches and pains in our bodies and of headaches for some days later.

The Commander enquired if I had been scared during the underwater shelling, to which my reply was "I nearly shit myself, Sir!"

"So did I, Knowles," he responded.

"A near death experience," I added.

He merely nodded .

A few days later, after scrounging a number of articles of RMS gear and commandeering a Canadian Dodge from an American army unit nearby, along with some articles of clothing that my boss laughingly said made us look like a couple of members of an ENSA concert party, we began our mine clearance work.

At the edge of the breakwater and partly awash we discovered a German mine with its parachute still intact and its tail fins, like a shark's, sticking out of the surface of the sea. We had no idea if it was magnetic, acoustic or anti-tippler, but it looked very sinister in its long, dull grey casing. I paddled up to my waist into the water to examine it and sat astride it. My boss then scared me to death when he said, "Knowles, I hope you have not got that bloody big American steel cigarette lighter in your pocket, it could actuate this mine and blow us to bloody bits!"

I presumed that he was joking – or was he?

I was alerted to a very distinctive smell that came from the mine, or should I say stink, for it seemed to be a mixture of old urine and chemicals. We noticed a slight, oily film floating around the mine. I was ordered to take cover behind the lighthouse, which was only thirty meters away from the bomb.

Commander Crabb started work, first applying 'the gag', an old fashioned motor horn that was pumped up by a bicycle pump until it was hard, then listening carefully for leaks that would allow the safety pin to rise. He shouted that the safety pin had popped home but was cursing madly in Mandarin when he could not move the keeper-ring. He asked for the long bronze (antimagnetic) keeper-ring spanner, which I had forgotten. With more Chinese cursing ringing in my ears, I set off at a run along the breakwater, then swimming a hundred yards across the basin entrance in order to retrieve the spanner from our Canadian transport vehicle. On my return, the Commander continued rendering the mine safe by removing the fuse. Later he apologised for cursing at me and stated that while I was away it gave him the opportunity to compose himself before tackling the dangerous task ahead, which seemed to take forever and included a number of cigarette breaks. At one stage I called from my sheltered position behind the lighthouse to enquire as to his progress, only to be answered by another expletive, spoken in Mandarin, a language I had often heard Commander Crabb use when under pressure. There followed an occasional burst of his well-known snorting laughter and finally a double clap of his hands, which I knew relieved him after rendering a mine safe.

I one day enquired if there was a great difference in working on a mine above or below water.

"No Knowles," he answered. "You can only make one mistake."

That evening we walked into the very badly damaged town of Leghorn. We dared not drive in because of the amount of Teller anti tank mines the Germans had placed in the roads. We had to search for a building as near as possible to the port that we could use for our HQ and spotted an ideal one in a very good position, just off the main road and close to the docks. It was a very imposing structure with a large wooden carved door painted red and while viewing it a man approached and stated that he was the owner and in a very truculent manner informed us that he had come to inspect the premises now that the German officers had moved on three days before. It had been his house, their club and a Bordello. He then demanded several thousand lira before we could enter. On being refused he slammed the door in our faces.

"Let's go Knowles," my boss stated. "We will deal with him later."

As we walked away and round a corner, a tremendous explosion took place and great masses of debris and the brothel's red wooden door flew past us and over our heads. Or friend must have flushed a toilet and actuated a farewell present from the previous German occupiers (presumably meant for us or the America troops).

From my very first meeting with my boss I recognised him as a man of outstanding ability and I very soon had admiration for his "guts" and technical know-how and also for the way he treated me as a man and not just a rating, for I am sorry to say, some officers in the Royal Navy in those days, especially the older commissioned officers, had a superiority complex which did not get the best from the men who they commanded. For all those reasons, I knew that I would follow him anywhere, no matter what the danger. I recall that when I first joined up with my boss he told me to speak up and make suggestions if it warranted it and never to ask "Permission to speak Sir?" I found this to be very refreshing too.

Just outside of Leghorn town we found new billets in a lovely old house named the Villa Banti, which had not been bombed or damaged. I shall always remember the surprise I got when entering the villa to see, hanging on the wall at the top of the wide stairway, a very large painting of a prancing white stallion. (I returned to the villa on a holiday in 1970 and was greeted enthusiastically by the Countess and family whose home it was). We were soon joined by a shore-based Bomb Disposal Unit under the command of Lieutenant Commander Phillips GM, MBE and Lieutenant Douglas, who seemed no worse from the head wound delivered by the German tank but who now was proudly sporting a vivid red scar above his right eye. Also a new member of their party was Gunner T (Warrant Officer) McLanachan. The entire length of the driveway up to the villa had a grass verge on each side and eventually every inch of it was covered with mines and bomb fuses of every type that we had found and rendered safe.

The Germans were now retreating north and the shelling of the port was easing off.

One of the members of the Bomb Disposal Unit was Able Seaman "Rex" King, who was tragically killed when we drove into a field to dispose of a mine by burning out the explosive. He had walked in front of the disposal lorry and very sadly stood on a concealed box mine, which almost blew off both of his legs. He was moaning loudly in pain and bleeding profusely. Moving forward on my hands and knees, I carefully crept up to his terribly injured body and gave him a morphine injection from the emergency pack I carried on my belt. While waiting for medical assistance to arrive, I knelt down alongside him in an effort to comfort him. I looked down at my legs and boots to find them saturated in his blood and this sent a signal to my brain and I found my whole body trembling and in a state of collapse. This tragic event seemed to trigger a latent fear in me, bringing home the fact that I had for a long time been involved in a very dangerous job and for the very first time in the war I cried and cried, the tears pouring down my face until one of the land mine disposal unit men said "come on now Baron, we understand."

We had a problem getting a stretcher to him because of the length of the grass around his body, which we were afraid might hide more deadly mines and we spent a considerable amount of time spiking the ground around him with our long slender commando knives to clear the area. It was then with sorrow that I saw his staring and bulging eyes close as he passed away and only after sweeping the area around him again and searching the ground very carefully were we able to recover his body. Later in the day we buried him in a little civilian cemetery at the rear of Leghorn town, where I cried again.

I later told my boss that I felt very embarrassed about breaking down and crying. He simply shook his head and said, "We have been fighting our fears far too long, Knowles and that was your safety valve. Don't worry, it could happen to me also, plus many more men."

One morning I answered a knock at the door to an Italian by the name of Vago Giari, who asked if could I give him a job diving. To my amazement he told me that he was an ex member of the 10th Flotilla. He had been one of the frogmen who attacked our shipping in Gibraltar but when Italy capitulated he had returned to his home in Leghorn. After interrogation at Naval HQ and given clearance he was accepted by us with open arms. Also that week, a very young and dapper Lieutenant Ventorini, who was also an ex member of the Gruppa Gamma, arrived at the villa to join us. He had been in Caserta at the allied HQ for interrogation and now that he had been cleared he wished to take part in our operations. This was subsequently to lead to a tragedy. I was ordered to take Lieutenant Ventorini to Naval HQ in Leghorn, under escort of a following vehicle containing two Royal Marines, on a road I had driven over several times. All at once there was a tremendous explosion. The escort vehicle behind me had driven over a Teller anti-tank mine which, by sheer fortune, had passed between the wheels of my jeep. Their vehicle was thrown into the air and both Marines were killed. The body of one had been flung out from the truck and cart-wheeled in the air; he was lying dead by the roadside, terribly mangled. The other, to my horror, was hanging suspended from a tangled and broken bunch of telephone wires, where he remained, swinging for a moment or two, before falling into a garden with an awful thud.

Ventorini, who was sitting beside me in the jeep, was visibly very shocked, for this was the first time he had experienced action and it resulted in him staggering up and down the road with head in his hands crying "Mamma Mia, Mamma Mia!" My immediate thought was 'I don't want this man as my buddy diver' and he never was my buddy, nor did I ever see him dive. This event left a lasting impression on my mind, as can be imagined, and for many days afterwards, when driving, I would flinch every time my vehicle encountered a bump on the road.

The harbour of Leghorn was now packed with American Liberty ships and freighters loaded with all the paraphernalia of war. Vago assisted me in searching the bottoms of the ships for magnetic mines. Also, through Vago Giari and Ventorini, intelligence was obtained that an Italian frogman group formerly of the 10th Flotilla, who had not yet surrendered and were under the command of Prince Borghese, were about to attack the shipping. Their HQ was at La Spezia, behind the German lines and only about thirty miles north of Leghorn.

Our diving now proved to be very, very difficult because orders had been issued that all ships must hang rolls of barbed wire around their hulls. These rolls hung as deep as three fathoms below the surface and were to deter enemy frogmen, but during a night dive my boss had badly torn the skin behind his left knee when he accidentally came into contact with one. This wire would prove to be a great deterrent for an enemy diver who was unaware of it in the dark and could lacerate his breathing bag, which could result in possible death.

I also found the water very, very cold, as it was November and I was still diving "naked" – that is, without a suit or, as we referred to it, as "bare-peg" and "the shrink" – words that anyone with the slightest knowledge of the male anatomy would understand for obvious reasons, although Vago had retained his own Italian frogman suit. We were still using DSEA breathing apparatus, which Vago hated, and some time later he appeared with two Italian 10th Flotilla oxygen sets, which were far superior to our British gear and allowed us to stay longer underwater, for the set carried dual oxygen bottles. The design I liked most of the Italian re-breather sets was the idea of a trigger instead of a wheel valve, which made the demand for oxygen fool-proof, especially when our hands were covered with oil, grease or very little feeling due to the cold that we were experiencing on every dive.

Commander Crabb had ordered a 24-hour watch on the breakwater and moles. One night an army sentry heard coughing, he challenged the noise, fired a shot and discovered two frogmen in wet shiny rubber suits, with arms raised in surrender. They turned out to be two enemy officers who had been delivered close into the port by fast motor boat. They had swum into the port towing a number of booby trap magnetic mines. We discovered that they were Lieutenants Malacarne and Sorgetti, and a little later a third swimmer, Lieutenant Bertoncin, was also captured towing mines. All these Italian frogmen had come from the HQ of Prince Borghese, the Black Knight, at the port of La Spezia to the north. It was like Gibraltar all over again.

Leghorn echoed to the roar of a small but very dangerous hand-made depth charges fashioned from tins of American C rations and thrown by the sentries on the moles, who ignited them by touching the fuse with a glowing cigarette end. We had carried out this practise from the moles in Gibraltar, but using Bully Beef tins. It was a strange experience for me to be diving in an attack without my Commander, who told us that he was away at Naval HQ Caserta. (I found out later that he had gone south to an Italian Military Hospital and was having emergency treatment for piles, but he was too embarrassed to tell anyone.)

For Vago Giari it was an extraordinary situation to be swimming around American ships in an allied port looking for mines placed by his old unit. Early one morning in January we arrived at the port to commence our usual search for limpet mines and, to our surprise, we found the inland part of the harbour covered with ice. I had never realised that it could get so cold on the coast of Italy in winter. I shuddered at the thought of diving "bare peg" but Vago assured me that he would search the ship alone, seeing that he would be wearing his frogman suit. I did not argue with him – as a matter of fact I was extremely grateful – and, borrowing oars from a rowing boat that was moored nearby, I broke enough ice to allow Vago to plunge beneath the surface. He was a wonderful diver and absolutely fearless and I admired him greatly. The result of his search was an 'all clear' – no mines.

In conversation with Vago, who was by now my diving buddy, we swapped stories of our time in Gibraltar and he also commented on his thoughts of meeting one of our party underwater. He also explained to me how he put a mine on one of our ships and I explained to him how I took it off! By now Vago and I had become very close friends and brothers in arms. As every diver knows, your diving partner becomes very important, as you rely on each other in any situation that arises. This friendship extended to invitations from Vago and his wife Liliana to Commander Crabb, Commander Phillips and I to dine with them at their home. We assisted with the meal by supplying corned beef and American C rations, which Liliana miraculously turned into a not to be forgotten feast.

I always thought that Vago's eagerness to assist us in our work was a result of the way that the Germans had treated his wife. Before the Allies had arrived in Leghorn the retreating Germans had started looting the town and when they attempted to enter her home she had resisted, which resulted in her being shot in the cheek and wounded.

During the enemy Frogmen attack I had given orders that the dropping of all explosive charges must cease while we, the search divers, were in the water, but the order was ignored and some fool sentry threw a charge very near to Vago as he surfaced. He dared not shout a warning in Italian or who knows what may have happened. He felt a violent pain in his back and again surrendered to the Allies. He was taken to a military hospital where he was detained for some time. Meanwhile I carried on searching alone for most of the night but found no mines. We had taken prisoners however. It was our victory.

After interrogating the prisoners we found the reason for the attack that had failed was to build up a supply of mines and equipment at a permanent sabotage centre and then attack shipping whenever they wished. The prisoners were found to be carrying 75,000 lire each (about £150), a small fortune in Italy in those days. Another member of the group, Lieutenant Pavone, had still to arrive. He would also be towing equipment for the sabotage team. This was information "squeezed" from the captured prisoners.

The following morning Pavone was arrested slinking out of the dockyard gate; the mines and gear that he had towed in I found in shallow water at the end of the breakwater. If this attempt had succeeded they planned to establish sabotage centres in every Allied port, which would seriously have slowed down the supplies to the Allied Army.

So ended the battle of Leghorn.

Commander Crabb and I now headed north, checking the areas of Viareggio and La Spezia, at the entrance of the river Sercio, where in World War 1 the idea and testing of two-man torpedoes was born. In the Italian Navy the men who volunteered had no title and were simply known as "Men of Sercio River".

Brigades of drunken partisans and booby-trapped mines were everywhere. We were invited to stay overnight in a camp occupied by a battalion of Japanese American troops of the 442nd Regimental Combat Team, who had previously fought at Cassino and whose motto was *Go For Broke*. Later they were to bravely face the Germans at the Gothic Line. Their camp was much preferable to sleeping in one of the ruined houses, where the most common form of booby-trap left by the retreating Germans was activated when the toilet was flushed and the whole house blew up. I shall never forget the kindness shown to us by Colonel Namanata, who provided us with real food and ice cream (when the Yanks go to war they provide everything!). I thought to myself that not many men can say they fought alongside the "Japanese".

It was reported that an old fashioned horned mine had been washed in by the tide and lay half buried in the sand on the beach at La Spezia, and we went to inspect it. I had noticed that the Commander did not seem his usual self and that his skin had taken on a strange tan. He was also in an unusual bad temper for most of the time, and I found myself being the "whipping boy" for everything that did not go right.

The mine, a very large German 'Y' type, lay on its side with half of the horn switches lying below the surface of the sand. The detonator, which had to be removed, was also buried and the compacted sand around it was as hard as concrete. But it was my job to remove it. After a sweaty half-hour later I had completed the task, enabling my boss to lie on his side and reach and remove the detonator. A number of fishermen were busy mending their nets and they had even strung them over the upper horns! The Commander cursed them severely in his usual Mandarin and when we had trouble removing the top-plate to burn out the explosive he savagely started to remove the corroded nuts, using a spanner and a large hammer. The fishermen sprinted away behind the sand dunes, for they had no idea that the mine was now safe. This was not normal Crabb behaviour. We eventually opened the mine and with Magnesium ribbon and cotton waste we burnt out the Hexonite explosive; it was like a giant torch.

In Savona, a small port further up the coast, a large mine was reported hanging from a derrick but submerged underwater. I dived to examine it and not to my surprise found a couple of strange wires attached to it, another booby trap! Not knowing how or wishing to render it safe, I attached a plastic charge to it and, retiring to a safe distance, blew the "booby" mine and derrick sky high.

Our next order was a great surprise – we were off on a flight by an American Dakota aeroplane, from Pisa airport to Marseilles in the South of France, to clear any mines found in the southern ports. In Marseilles harbour it was reported to us that the Germans, before retreating, had lowered what the witness described has a very long cylinder underwater against the harbour and entrance wall and underneath the giant crane above. We dived to examine it to discover that it was a German 'George', lying in deep mud that was hiding the area of access to the detonator. My boss tried to clear the area but found the mine too heavy to turn over, so we dived together and with our combined strength and the aid of ropes tied to an iron ladder that was permanently erected into the harbour wall below a very large bollard, we managed to turn it over to expose the cover plate on its rear and allow my boss the very terrifying job of rendering the mine safe.

"Ok Knowles, get clear, a couple of hundred yards at least, and remove all the men sitting on the seaward side of the wall fishing… and, by the way, never let me move a mine like that again, we could have been blown to bloody bits!" said the Commander.

It seemed that, unbeknown to me, the mine might have been fitted with an anti-tippler booby trap and I quickly came to the conclusion that my boss was going out of his mind. He had been acting strangely for some time. I shook my head in disbelief and decided that in future I would question everything we were doing. On this particular mine I did not hear his wonderful snorting laugh and the double clap of his hands when he had completed his task.

We arrived in Port Sete, in a battered old taxi, to find the whole fishing community pleading with us to remove a mine that the Germans had placed in the entrance next to the wall of the harbour, which was blocking in the fishing fleet. This mine, another German 'George', had been placed on the deck of a motor boat and sunk. After diving and appraising the situation, we found the 'George' had been heavily booby-trapped and would be impossible to render safe, so we decided that the best scenario was to blow it up in situ. When we informed the Mayor and fishermen of our intentions, they threw up their arms in violent protest – we had not taken into account that only a few yards away on the quay was the statue of the Virgin Mary, "patroness" of the port and now well within range of what would be a violent explosion.

After much discussion and another inspection we dived again and again to attach very heavy ropes and wire cables to the motor boat and the other ends to a very old steam-roller, with the intention of dragging the boat and mine into the centre of the basin. This attempt proved too much for the ancient roller, so we asked the Mayor if they could include a couple of horses. He answered by a shake of his head and informed us that the last horse had been eaten at least a year before. Then, in a very loud voice, he demanded help from about a hundred of the fishermen's families and bystanders who were watching our feeble efforts, and as one they arose and started to assist by pulling on the ropes. What a scene! Men, women and children, smoke, steam and sparks belching from the funnel of the old engine and roars of encouragement. At last the motorboat broke clear of the muddy bottom and with a great cheer from the heaving crowd it began to move into the centre of the basin and away from the beloved Virgin Mary. We dived and removed all the ropes, wire cables and shackles, then the Commander placed a countermining charge under the mine, which now lay about 30ft below the surface. We connected the detonator to the charge and fired. The result was only a loud thud. I had also prepared to dive, but the Commander refused to allow me, because the mine would probably now be in a delicate state after being so badly disturbed. (I think he must have remembered the mine that we tackled in Marseilles). He dived again and placed another charge against the mine, and once more we attempted to detonate. This time the mine and our explosive erupted with a tremendous roar and the explosion echoed around the basin. The resulting dead fish floating on the surface were eagerly collected by the crowd ... but again I heard no snorting laugh or clap of satisfaction from my boss.

The port was now open for the fishing fleet to resume their work and supply more food to the almost starving people in the area. I was elated by our success but my boss seemingly could not recall what had been happening during the last few hours. This was not the first time he had displayed a lapse of memory – the way we had handled the

Marseilles mine was another example. Why it didn't detonate I will never know. We had been bloody lucky![10]

The very same evening Commander Crabb collapsed. He was said to have "broken down" and was admitted to a French military hospital suffering from jaundice and exhaustion. He later admitted to me that he had cried. His "safety valve" had lifted, just like mine, and it was all for the better. He was to remain there in hospital for a number of weeks. While visiting him, I again asked him if he could arrange for me to get or sit for a promotion. He promised again that he would do this for me, but nothing ever came of my request.

It was now mid-December and I was joined by a temporary new boss, a Sub-Lieutenant Bull RNVR, and together we carried on searching the ports as far away as Port Vendre near the Spanish border. I think he suffered as much as me when he saw my almost naked body plunging into the cold sea and when I rapidly burst to the surface he always repeated the same thing.

"Bloody Hell, Knowles! Bloody Hell! How do you do it?" and I always replied through chattering teeth, "Duty sir. Duty with pertinacity and endurance." This always made him laugh and comment "Good man!"

On our journey along the French coast we travelled on a battered ex-German military motorbike and sidecar, which initially had three flat tyres and which we had bought, or rather "forced" from a farmer who was wearing the jacket of a French military uniform. This purchase cost us a small amount of cash plus a navy Pusser's blanket.

---

[10] Throughout the whole of my diving career with Commander Crabb I am happy to report that – amazingly, when you consider all that we went through – only one diver was lost, and that was Lieutenant Hood in Gibraltar, although I still vividly recall the removing and handling of that mine in Marseilles, where we will never know how close we came to death. Indeed, a few years after the war, when the Commander and I were reminiscing about our deeds together, I casually mentioned the German George mine at Marseilles, whereupon I was curtly and loudly told, with some embarrassment, to "Shut up Knowles!"

We found it very difficult to find food for days until one morning we came across a military barracks at Perpignan; it was occupied by a few French troops and a very large number of members of the Maquis, or French partisans. We asked the chef for a meal but were refused point blank and told to go and find our own. I began to hate the Vichy French. We "found" our food by creeping behind his kitchen where, in a pen, we saw a few chickens. I grabbed a couple and shared them with a grateful old lady whose house we came upon a number of miles down the road. She cooked them for the three of us and served them with a very good wine.

I was still diving "bare peg" and each dive was gut-wrenching with considerable pain due to the severe cold water and I made each search very rapid and welcomed the rough and thorough towelling down when I surfaced. While awaiting the discharge of the Commander from hospital I had found a nice billet in Marseilles and my time was spent with Sub Lieutenant Bull, checking the harbour and any ships that were berthed there and reporting to my boss, who told me to try and get a flight back to Pisa, but without result.

My New Year's Eve of 1944 was a very lonely one and I was later informed that I was, apart from the two officers, the only sailor of the Royal Navy in the south of France at that time. In all the months that we spent in this area amongst the Vichy French I got the impression that we, the British, were not welcome and they were, to a man, very Pro-German, the only exception being the kind old lady who had cooked the chickens for us and who had sent us on our way with many blessings and a *bon voyage*.

I eventually returned to Leghorn and the Villa Banti, by fishing boat, many weeks later. To my great surprise, Vago was waiting for me with a belated Christmas present – my very own two-piece Italian diving suit, complete with pure silk one-piece underwear (the end of 'the shrink'!). Together we returned to our routine dawn dives, looking for a chance limpet mine under the American supply ships.

My friendship with Vago and his family grew and was to continue long after the war, when I visited them in Leghorn and during one visit he kindly gave to me his decoration miniatures (two silver Al Valor Militare and three crosses Valor de Guerra). The ribbons are surmounted by a golden octopus. I was also given his unit's shield (Comsubin) with crocodile and anchor. COMando SUBacquei INcurson is the equivalent to the British S.B.S. And the American Seals. I also have in my possession Vago Giari's personal account, etitled *SEI MISSIONI DI GUERR* in which he describes the plan to attack the shipping in New York harbour. Vago and I spent many hours chatting about our experiences and the battle against each other in Gibraltar and we each bragged of our special achievements underwater.

Vago Giari had volunteered in July 1940 to join the Italian Diving and Frogmen Group. In December of that year he was ordered to go to the city of La Spezia were, after undergoing a medical, only 11 were men were chosen from many dozens of volunteers. He was then transferred to the Naval Academy in Livorno, to take part for many weeks in a diving and diving instructor's course (a tremendous difference to my introduction to diving in the Gibraltar Underwater Working Party).

He then went to Palermo, to recover a sunken motor torpedo boat; this was a very harrowing job as Vago, along with three other divers, was working among the dead who had gone down with their ship.

Returning to Livorno in 1942, Vago was asked if he would like to join a group of Naval Saboteurs and, after training in the art of sabotage, the group were called to the office of Prince Borghese, shown how magnetic mines worked, and then he wished them well.

Vago and two others left Livorno in a car driven by a German; they all wore civilian clothes. A Captain Marino was in charge until they were met by a smuggler, who had been paid by the Italian government to take them over the Pyrenees. They then transferred to an Italian car sent from the Italian embassy in Madrid. The frogmen were taken to Cadiz and stayed a short time aboard an Italian oil tanker. Three others had also made the same journey and another six had entered Spain by sea at Barcelona. They then moved to a villa near Algeciras where, a short time later, a truck arrived from La Spezia, bringing small rubber dinghies, wet suits, lifejackets, mines and other essential equipment. (It was absolutely amazing that the Spanish a "neutral country" allowed these blatant operations to take place.) They then hid the mines in sacks of coal and their rubber diving suits in mattresses and transferred all their equipment to another villa. This operation was organised by Engineer Pistone, who was the Italian Vice Consul.

It was from this villa, the Villa Carmella, on the outskirts of the town of La Linea and close to the sea (as we were to later discover) that the Italian frogmen launched their attacks on the Allied shipping in the bay of Gibraltar. One of the ships Vago sunk was the 1,700 ton *Meda*, for which he was awarded a gold medal. It was also from the villa Carmella that Vago and the other Italian frogmen had watched us diving to remove the mines that they had attached to the ships. What a motley crew we must have looked to them, diving with no wetsuits, summer and winter and going down in only swimming trunks and weighted plimsolls, wasting many hours searching ships that they knew had no mines attached to them, although they told me that our tenacity was admired very much by them.

Vago spent some time in Seville and then returned to the Villa Carmella after spending several days aboard the *Olterra* in the Port of Algeciras. Now Engineer Romanino and his wife were living in the villa to give them a cover and an appearance of normality. The frogman group carried out many more attacks on allied shipping before returning to Italy by plane, Vago was greeted with the news that he had been awarded his second gold medal. Vago and his companions then went on to attack shipping in the ports of Tunisia.

While my boss was still in hospital in France, I, on several occasions, accompanied Commander Phillips to the Dockyard in Leghorn to assist him and his Bomb Disposal Team in the clearance of hundreds of Teller mines from the quayside. Many of these mines had been cemented into the ground to disguise them, leaving only a couple of millimetres of the mine top plate cover protruding, and removing them involved hours and hours of hammering and chiselling, with extreme care.

A large mine was reported dumped by the Germans just outside the entrance to the harbour of Porto Ferrio on the Isle of Elba, which involved us making a mad dash by jeep to Piombino and a boat trip across to the island. This trip was almost my last, for while searching for the reported mine in almost 70ft of water I was rendered unconscious by oxygen poisoning. Very fortunately I floated to the surface and was spotted and dragged aboard the nearby boat. I later discovered that my accident was due to my breathing bag being perforated on one of my earlier dives under the barbed wire in Leghorn; the seawater had ruined the Protosorb granules that "cleaned" the carbon dioxide I exhaled. To add insult to injury, subsequent searches proved that no mine existed. This operation had been very difficult, for the entire area for miles around was covered in sea grass, a great green meadow about two meters high, swaying in the current.

During a further dive in that area I was surprised to find myself surrounded by a pod of about twenty dolphins, who darted out of this wonderful green forest to investigated me thoroughly but never showing any sign of aggression and together we had a playful time as they danced around me and I thought that, with music, it could have been a ballet. The piercing noise of their communications and their rapid clicks seemed to overcome everything around me and I felt bonded and at one with them. As swiftly as they had appeared, and to my very great disappointment, they had gone. "Oh! I wish I could have just half of their diving ability!" I thought to myself. "Not to mention their other remarkable and mysterious senses." The dolphins were the first living creatures I had seen underwater over the last couple of years, but this was understandable, considering the amount of underwater explosions that took place around Gibraltar. I later heard that, a year after hostilities ceased, dolphins were again spotted around the Rock.

Leaving Elba, I returned to the Villa Banti in Leghorn to find that the lighthouse I had taken cover behind many months before had disappeared. It had been destroyed by a massive long-delay booby-trap mine and its remains, great blocks of stone, had been hurled by the explosion over the entire port area and into parts of the nearby town. I shivered a little as I counted my blessings, for my luck was certainly holding. It could have exploded at any time while my boss and I were there, unaware of the great amount of explosive beneath our feet.

Commander Crabb Crabb. eventually returned and made a signal to Caserta HQ that he was back in business. The Allied armies had been bogged down during the winter, rather like himself, and it was now March 1945 and he was eager to get back to work. An order arrived from Caserta, ordering us to the great port of Genoa, where we discovered the largest booby-trap we had ever seen. Commander Crabb and I dived to inspect a normal-looking dry dock, which was flooded to about 25ft in depth, where, to our amazement, we discovered lines and lines of horned mines, standing side by side on the bottom of the dock, like lines of soldiers at attention. We discovered that a German minelayer had unloaded its entire cargo of mines to facilitate a repair before they retreated and instead of reloading they decided to put them to use and stem the Allied advance. We double- and then treble-counted this deadly trap; our final tally amounted to 84. In addition we discovered that all the mines were wired together and that furthermore, sitting on the parapets of the dry docks walls, were shelves of further mines, totalling over

100 more. With great urgency we dived from mine to mine in an attempt to trace the important wire or wires that would have activated them and thus brought about a tremendously destructive explosion that could have resulted in many deaths and destroyed the port and part of the city.

We did find four main wires leading to the surface but each of them led in a different direction and lay under massive heaps of bomb debris.

"A tricky one Knowles. We must find the trigger that actuates this massive bomb," said the Commander.

I was ordered to contact the Military Police, who had very sensibly stayed many hundreds of yards away, to tell them to clear the entire dockyard. I was recalled to the scene and, to my great surprise, Commander Crabb thanked me and shook my hand. This was the first time that I had seen and sensed that my boss was suffering pressure.

"Every action I take I shall write down in this leather-backed notebook. This is a serious situation. You must now take cover and do not move until I call you or until..."

Nothing more needed to be said and I left him with a heavy heart. A very firm and quiet friendship had developed between us and while we had worked together on many mines, suddenly all around felt foreboding and sinister. As I walked away he called, "Chin up Baron, it will be alright!"

I took shelter behind the great bulk of the Italian Aircraft Carrier *Roma*, which was floating in a dock nearby, empty and deserted. I lit my pipe and settled down to a long wait but was shockingly interrupted by an underwater explosion nearby. Two Italian youths had crept into the area and were throwing German 'stick' grenades into another flooded dock nearby in attempt to stun fish to the surface. I warned them away by firing a couple of rounds at them from my .38 revolvers and they were then rounded up by the military police.

I was brought to attention about an hour later when the Commander's voice demanded help to lift a very large block of concrete.

"Bloody hell, Sir! We can't lift that up!" I said when I saw it.

"There is no such word in this game," he said. "Now look around you man and bring a large baulk of timber."

Over one hour later we had moved the concrete to discover a junction box with three wires leading into it.

"Bring me the bolt-cutters Knowles – and a towel."

Relieved at the sound of his voice I raced round the bow of the *Roma* to get the articles he required and returning, met what looked like a scarecrow; he was smothered in dirt and brick dust, rivulets of sweat had scoured his face and his uniform was torn and ruined by black oil. I presumed that I must look the same. He took the cutters from me and said with a grin, "Tidy yourself up man! If Chief Petty Officer Thorpe was here he would put both of us on a charge!" We both laughed aloud. "Another bloody ten minutes of hell Knowles!" he stated, with his snorting laugh and another double clap of his hands – the action and comment he always made after a job, no matter how long the operation had taken.

"Where is the leather-backed book Sir?" I asked.

He shook his head and shrugged his shoulders, and we grinned at each other. We had managed to trace the main wires under the debris and rendered the mines safe and the dockyard was now open again.

A couple of days later we were informed that a search boat manned by Italian dockyard workers had snagged an object underwater in the channel at the entrance to the docks but had failed to buoy it, resulting in my boss and I swimming for hundreds and hundreds of yards just above the seabed in a sort of grid pattern in an attempt to locate it, very thankful once again for the fins we were now wearing. Unfortunately the visibility was bad, but coming out of the gloom I almost bumped into a very large, dome-shaped metal object, the like of which I had never seen before. In our talk prior to diving we had agreed that if we spotted anything we would inform each other by striking our diving knives against any hard object at hand, resulting in a clanging noise that would carry clearly underwater to inform each other of our result. This I did, on the very large dome, resulting in a sound resembling a peal of church bells. I continued striking until I felt the presence of Commander Crabb just above me, signalling me franticly to stop. As we did not wear helmets, I removed my breathing mouthpiece and, moving almost face-to-face with him so we could lip-read, I mouthed, "Is it a mine?" He responded with a deliberate nod of the head, "Yes, yes!" and signalled me to surface. Underwater voice communication had not yet been invented.

When we had both surfaced he exclaimed, "Bloody hell Knowles! You have found an OYSTER MINE!" Although I had never heard of it, this particular type of German mine had been discovered before and was well known in the UK, but Commander Crabb stated that he had no information on how to tackle it. It was, he said, a real beauty – pressure, magnetic, acoustic, fitted with photoelectric cells and anti-tippler.

"I must make some urgent phone calls," he concluded.

A couple of days later I contracted violent stomach pains and was rushed to a military hospital on the outskirts of Genoa city, where I was detained for a number of days. I thought it was food poisoning but the doctor diagnosed my problem as stomach cramps due to underwater pressure. During this stay in hospital, Lieutenant Gerald Shirley RNVR and Lieutenant Joe Howard RNVR had arrived to assist my boss and together they rendered the oyster mine safe. Both these officers had previously taken a two-week course at HMS *Excellent*, the Diving School at Portsmouth, using the standard diving suit with large copper helmet and our gear was new to them, but after a couple of practice dives they did OK in our DSEA oxygen breathing sets. I believe that both these officers were later decorated.

Orders arrived for us to leave Genoa and head to Venice, but the Commander decided that a little diversion was in order, so we headed north-east through the Dolomites and visited lakes Como and Garda. We were not like the regular tourists of previous years; no grand hotels for us. We slept on and under our wagon, but did manage to obtain a large bowl of spaghetti and meatballs for breakfast and later scrounged a boat ride on the lake as far as the north shore. No money was exchanged – only thanks and our hands shaken vigorously. The beauty of the area and the kindness of its people were to leave a lasting impression and I was to return in later years to enjoy many happy holidays skiing in the area.

We entered Venice and the island of Le Vignole, the base of the 10th Flotilla where we found the workshops and laboratories intact and many Italian divers there. In charge were two sergeants – Berri and Froguglia – who stated that they all wished to surrender. We were later joined on the island by Lieutenant Commander Marsloe and his American Intelligence Unit. Venice had to be cleared of mines and every diver of the remaining Italian 10th Flotilla volunteered for the massive task ahead to save their beloved city.

On the island I met Dr Moscatelli, also a diver, who had been based at the Villa Carmella in Spain and was also the captain of the *Oltterra* (the ship with the underwater door). It turned out that he had often masqueraded as a Spaniard in a bum-boat selling oranges to the soldiers on the anchored troop ships and had often been within a few metres of us and the intelligence he gained of our activities was passed to both the Italian and German HQs. He recognised us immediately and even noted that the Commander had shaved off his beard. The removal of the beard had been an accident in Gibraltar, when with an absent mind he had attempted to light his cigarette over a leaking oxygen booster pump. The result was a flash of flame and the smell of singed hair ... followed by a lengthy Chinese curse. We could hardly recognise him the following day for he had completely shaved off the remnants. When asked by anyone who was not aware of the accident he would state that his beard had been interrupting the entrance to his mouthpiece and breathing pipe.

Dr Moscatelli proved to be a most likeable fellow. The most unforgettable character I met, however, was Commander Angelo Belloni, the First World War submariner and inventor who had conceived the whole idea of frogmen and the Tenth Light Flotilla. He had invented most of its gear and persuaded Mussolini to let him form an underwater attack group. On the arm of his shirt he wore the badge of the Tenth Light Flotilla; a skull with a rose in its jaw. He was a distinctive elderly gentleman with a shaven head, extremely deaf and spoke broken English with a very loud voice. He and I kept in touch until his death, a number of years after the war, and I always welcomed his letters in well typed English, the sheets embossed with his emblem of the scull and rose.

The Germans had laid mines close to the junction of the Giadecca and Grand Canals. If minesweepers were to be brought in to flush them out, a possible explosion could damage St Marks square the church of St Marks and the Doge's Palace. However, they were controlled mines and non-magnetic and we and the team of Italian divers soon rendered them safe and removed them.

The Italians took great pride in their work and the clearance jobs were very thorough. The longest search period was the examination of the railway bridge and it culverts that stretched between the mainland and the Venice islands. Two torpedo warheads had been placed under the Bridge of Sighs; they were of the non-magnetic type and, diving from a gondola, these were coolly rendered safe by Commander Crabb.

A magnetic-acoustic mine had also been reported in the vicinity of an Italian tanker that the Germans had used as a reservoir for fresh water in the area; she was moored some distance from the quay. The tanker and drinking water had to be saved for the use of the city, which ruled out the use of a minesweeper, as it could not explode the mine without blowing up the tanker as well. So it would have to dealt with the hard way.

But first the mine had to be traced. The water in Venice was filthy and dark and our usual practice in such conditions was to lay a weighted grid over the area, in order to search methodically. The group of Italian divers working with us considered this routine too slow and were ready to dive en-mass and search blindly but Commander Crabb would not allow this. Instead, in almost complete darkness, he and I searched close to the bottom until, after some considerable time and the replacing of the grid to different locations, he scraped over an obstruction that turned out to be the mine. Most of it was buried in the mud, except for the tail, which protruded upwards.

We did not feel that we had a hope of rendering it safe underwater and the tanker could not be moved, for this would activate the mine and not only destroy a 7,000-ton ship but also block the main canal. There had been a similar mine in the lagoon at Le Vignole, which the Commander had successfully dealt with by placing a charge that had blown off it its tail without setting off the main explosive and we were considering whether we could try the same routine now. However, some hours had passed and the captain of the tanker, becoming impatient, decided to risk moving his ship. He had been informed not to use his engines, so tried to get clear of the mine by hauling on the anchor that lay well ahead of his bow, but the moment the tanker moved, the mine exploded. Luckily, no damage was done to the ship, the brunt of the explosion having been absorbed by the thick mud in which the mine was lying.

Reports were coming in from members of the public who had seen the Germans place mines in the canals in various parts of the city and I will always recall one that was placed under the Ponti Tetta, a bridge that was famous because of the many prostitutes who gathered there, many of whom bared their breasts (tetas), a practise that had continued for centuries. When the Italian divers found and rendered the mine safe, the girls watching nearby cheered and, as one, bared their breasts in gratitude, for they knew that the victorious Eighth Army would soon be entering Venice and the bridge had now been rendered safe for use by their many forthcoming "customers".

During our stay on the island of Le Vignole we were visited one evening by Signora Visinti, the widow of Lieutenant Visinti, accompanied by Lieutenant Eugenio Wolk. Her husband had been the frogman who died in Gibraltar when piloting a two-man torpedo. She wanted to meet us and find out for herself how her husband had died and how we had buried him. The memory of the meeting weighed upon us both. British wartime propaganda often chose to portray the Italian armed forces as cowards, mostly as a consequence of the thousands of troops who surrendered in North Africa because they did not wish to carry on fighting. But this was certainly not the case with the Italian diving groups, who were brave and dedicated warriors. All of our Underwater Working Party admired them greatly, for we knew what it was like "down there."

Peace was slow to come to Venice, but fortunately the beautiful city had escaped much of the hunger and damage that had been inflicted on the rest of Italy. During our work in Venice we were clearing mines on the island of Moreno and learned that the world-famous glassworks, which had been operating there for centuries, had never closed during the war. My boss took the opportunity of purchasing a dozen wine glasses and having each one engraved with a crab. It was fascinating to watch the wonderful artists at work, using the skills passed down though their forefathers for hundreds of years.

Back in England, my father, a widower, had remarried and gone to live with his new wife, but had failed to inform me of his new address. Nevertheless, one morning I was informed by Commander Crabb that my father had written to Admiral Mountbatten, complaining that the war was now over and that his son "had not been seen or heard from for three years". As a result, I was ordered to return to my depot in Plymouth. I received this news with a heavy heart, for I was enjoying the work and the adrenalin rushes and really had no wish to return. But return I must.

My Commander and I exchanged our farewells and I boarded a train with hard wooden seats that took three days and nights to cross France and reach the port of Dieppe, from whence I was ferried by fishing boat across the Channel. It would be several years before I was reunited with my boss Commander Crabb, a man who I held in high esteem and with whom I felt a mutual bond.

On my arrival at my depot in Devonport I was informed that the King had been graciously pleased to award me The British Empire Medal (Military Division). I sent a telegram to my father informing him of my award and that I was coming home on leave, also the exact time that I would arrive at Preston Railway Station. The telegram was sent from a little sub post office in Devonport and when I passed the written message to the little elderly man behind the counter he insisted on shaking my hand said, "*I* will pay for this telegram sailor."

To my great disappointment, dismay and sadness my father was not at the station to greet me. When I eventually arrived at his home he embraced me and, with tears rolling down his face and sobbing on my shoulder, said "Sydney, you know me". I was puzzled and did not understand but was damned if I would ask for an explanation. He passed away many years ago. We were never close and I wonder if his strange behaviour was a scar that his experiences of war had left upon him.

On the second day of my leave I was introduced to a friend of my father who was accompanied by his very pretty daughter Joan, who was a serving WAAF and still wearing her uniform although on discharge leave. It was 'love at first sight' and within the month, by special license that cost seven shillings and sixpence, we were married at Preston

Registry Office (we wanted a church marriage but that would not be possible unless I converted to Catholicism).

"It won't last," I sensed that I could hear them whispering, but it did – for forty-seven years until Joan's death in Spain.

Back in my depot in Devonport, in 1946 I once again applied to sit for promotion, which was granted as long as I put in some time at sea to familiarise myself with engine and boiler room procedure and I was drafted to the aircraft carrier HMS *Victorious,* later to be nicknamed *The Honeymoon Ship*. Her hangars had been stripped and rigged out with hundreds of beds and bunks in preparation for a trip out to Australia and the Far East to collect Aussie Brides, Nuns, Priests, Missionaries, etc, who had all been trapped by the war with Japan. On the outward bound voyage we had onboard a number of Jesuit priests who were going East to replace the returning members of the Brotherhood. This was ideal for my conversion to Catholicism and I spent most of my spare time on the voyage being tutored by one of the Jesuit Fathers. I informed him of my refusal to pray with the little Irish priest and Commander Crabb when we visited St Peters in Rome because of my feelings about what I and thousands of other people had suffered, and he quietly replied, "And so did Jesus Christ."

We sailed south to the Mediterranean, then through the Suez Canal and into the Indian Ocean. The ship felt ghostly with no roar of aircraft taking off or landing and only a very small to crew necessary to operate her. We had been at sea for a month. Sydney Australia was our first pick up point and the scene on the dockside was amazing with hundreds of exited and chattering women struggling to get over the gangway in order to be first aboard. Priority was given to mothers with tiny tots and babes in arms. Most of the women were in their late teens and early twenties and amongst them were a number of volunteer nurses to accompany them during the voyage to England.

Before sailing to our next port (Singapore) an order was issued that no member of the crew would be allowed in the hangars or flight deck areas unless by special permission or in an emergency. The enormous flight deck looked like the Bondi beach at Sydney, with lines and lines of beautiful girls lying on blankets and an occasional deckchair, most of them scantily dressed in order to sunbathe.[11] I doubt if a scene like this had ever been seen on a Royal Navy ship or would ever be seen again. It was obvious that officers were not being classed as crew for on the long balmy evenings they could be seen strolling along the flight deck with one of the women or "Sheilas" by their side. No shore leave was given in Singapore to our crew or to the women aboard but it was not long before I saw Japanese prisoners of war on the dockside carrying suitcases and baggage belonging to a number of catholic nuns, who were to live aboard in a specially prepared area of privacy.

We took on fuel and supplies then headed out to the South China Sea for our next port of call, Hong Kong, where we anchored below The Peak, the mountain that towers above the city, and to my surprise HMS *Belfast* the City Class cruiser was in port and tied up alongside the docks. I knew that aboard her was my cousin Bill Hughlock, a Royal Marine and a survivor of the battleship *Royal Oak* which was torpedoed and sunk by a U-Boat in Scapa Flow, north of Scotland in the Orkney Isles, early on in the war. I had not seen him for over six years, so I asked for shore leave and explained the circumstances, along with the fact that I was due to be baptized into Catholicism at the Wha Yan College. My request was granted and I was given a 24-hour pass. When Bill and I met, he said, "When I was told that I had a family visitor from ashore, I said 'There are no bloody Chinks in our family'!"

"Love will find a way" so the saying goes, and it did, for on the long, idle trip back to England the order of 'no fraternizing' seemed to have disappeared and at night in the many

[11] Another order was that no children would be allowed on deck for danger of them falling overboard.

dark nooks and crannies of the tremendously large ship, many couples were busy "coupling". A night patrol was organised to order women back into the hanger if they were found outside its perimeter.

A number of hilarious scenes occurred while sailing through the Suez Canal, prompted by the very short distance between the crowded flight deck and the shore in some places where Arab men both young and old, seemingly driven into a frenzy of excitement at the sight of so many scantily-dressed women, kept pace with the ship, shouting "Missy! Missy!" whilst lifting the fronts of their jalabas to expose themselves. Our answer to this was to open the upper deck lockers where all the ships vegetables were stowed and pelt the "flashers" with fusillades of potatoes to try and drive them away. This had little effect in most cases, however, for the spuds were simply gathered up in the folds of their raised jalabas to provide their next meal, an activity encouraged by the Arab women stood watching nearby.

The Honeymoon Ship arrived in Portsmouth to be greeted by many eager husbands, most wearing Demob Suits, and accompanied by mothers-in-law from all over the UK. A Royal Marine Band played *Waltzing Matilda* and in most cases there were scenes of happy reunion, although not everyone was happy, for many tears were shed by those "brides" who had recently transferred their affections from the man they had married in the Far East to one of the crew of the *Victorious* who she had possibly known longer and perhaps more intimately than her husband. Many hours later, embarrassing scenes were still taking place, with husbands, in some cases, pleading for their wives to step ashore. Some onlookers seemed to find these scenes hilarious but to me it was not funny to see a weeping man with a broken heart and a mother trying to comfort her son while screaming abuse at her erstwhile daughter-in-law who would not leave the ship.

But I had my own marriage to think about and was eager to tell my wife the happy news of my conversion to Catholicism. We were married at the church of St Joseph, near to our home, on my very next leave.

I was missing my diving work, for it had been my whole life for many years, so I put in a request to join the diving school at Plymouth. I found the underwater work familiar, for I had experienced the wearing of Seibe Gorman's Standard diving dress, with big lead-weighted boots and copper helmet, when burning off the mines from the bilge keels of ships in Gibraltar. It was good to be back underwater again and I experienced my first 150ft dive under the watchful eye of Chief Petty Officer Diver Jack Diamond, our instructor.

On completion of the course I was drafted to South Queens Ferry in Scotland and HMS *Lochinvar*, where the Royal Navy was to train its new Clearance Diving Team to specialise in searching for and disposing of underwater bombs and mines. I felt at home again and the old fire was back in my belly, for I was in the company of men after my own heart.

Officers and other ratings enquired constantly about my experiences during the war and I was able to convey to them how Commander Crabb and I had gone about our work rendering mines safe in Gibraltar, France and Italy, both describing the various types of mines we found and the methods by which we disposed of them.

I have been recently in contact with Lieutenant Commander John Gratton, who was the first to command some of the men I helped to train, who then went on to serve in the Mediterranean Clearance Diving Team based in Malta. John Gratton is at present in Tobermory, searching with a group of civilian divers for a Spanish galleon sunk in 1588. My own connection with this galleon I will relate later.

5. Postwar Mine & Bomb Disposal … and a Treasure Hunt

The war was now over but there was still a tremendous amount of work to be done in all the ports in Great Britain. For the previous six years Hitler had been dropping bombs and mines all over the country, many of them falling into the docks and harbours. A good number of these did not explode and were lying in the mud in a very dangerous condition, posing a great threat to the movement of shipping. In response the Admiralty began to train the first group of specialist Clearance Divers.

I tried to reunite with Commander Crabb but had no success, for he was away on some type of secret work for Admiral Mountbatten in a research lab at Bushey Park, details of which I was only to discover some time later.

I was now diving in London's dockland – at the Royal Albert and Tilbury docks – with a new boss, Lieutenant John Crawford RN, who I discovered had a brain as sharp as a knife. To prove it, when on the bridge of HMS *Dipper* sailing south out of the Forth, he stated that from scratch he would memorize the Morse Code completely before we arrived in Portsmouth. Before we opened the signals book to check him he admitted that he knew the letters SOS and that he did not want to cheat. We were amazed when he completed the challenge successfully.

John introduced me into The Royal Navy Ski and Mountaineering Club and when on leave in Scotland we climbed a lot of peaks together, especially on the Cuillin Mountains on the Isle of Skye and along the very exposed areas of Scurr Nan Gillean. He also invited me, along with two other members of the navy club, to tackle the Ben Nevis north face, which John described as 'the dark side' and it turned out to be a hard scramble on a rope with a fair amount of exposure. I found it thrilling but, by the end of the day, a tough climb. On one memorable day, in a blinding snowstorm and the whole mountain covered in ice, we successfully climbed the famous Cobbler Peak at the head of Loch Long, overlooking the beautiful little area of Arrochar. In normal circumstances it's a fairly easy climb to sit on the boulder at the top, but when the whole of Ben Arthur is snowed in it's another matter completely.

Our reason for being at the head of Loch Long with HMS *Dipper* was to recover a special and secret torpedo that had been fired in a test run from the submarine base at the northern end of Loch Long at Faslane but it had not been successful. We trawled, dived and found our 'big fish' in about 12 metres of water, buried nose deep in a bank of very fine shale and pebbles and in water of beautiful clarity. I sat astride it and immediately the memory of the German George mine in Leghorn returned to me with Commander Crabb's warning of "that bloody big cigarette lighter in your pocket Knowles". I burst out laughing and almost spat out my breathing mouthpiece. I had come through a lot since then. Since returning to the UK I was now wearing a diving suit of the "Port Party" type, designed originally for the searching of mines in ports and harbour bottoms and my "Bare Peg" days had long gone, but I still felt the "nip" of a Scottish Loch.

I had only been with the new party for a week when my new CO sent for me to inquire why I had not had any promotion. I informed him of the numerous requests I had put in to Commander Crabb and of my four-month trip to the Far East aboard the Aircraft Carrier HMS *Victorious* to familiarize myself with the boiler and engine rooms and he shook his head, mumbling, "he didn't want to lose you". Within a couple of weeks I had been promoted to the dizzy heights of Leading Stoker Mechanic and that rank stayed with me until I left the Navy, for it would have meant leaving my diving division and returning to engineering to obtain further promotion and this I was not prepared to do, for by now diving was my life and I was happy and contented.

Our working conditions in the river Thames were the worst I had ever experienced, for although the water was only twenty to thirty feet deep it overlaid a layer of liquid mud about ten to twelve feet in thickness and when I descended into it on a trial dive the visibility was nil and I could not move my limbs more than a couple of inches in any direction for the mud had grasped me. We described the conditions as "black custard". Searching by eye was completely out of the question and swimming or crawling along the bottom was impossible, so we solved this problem by dragging heavy weighted ropes through the mud in order to snag any object it came across and then diving down and pulling our body forcibly down the rope and clawing through the very thick mud to feel by hand what we had snagged.

There were many surprises. Under the arms of the cranes along the dock sides where ships were unloaded had become, over the years, a vast tip of articles accidentally dropped. Our party found a couple of American Jeeps, many army motorbikes, many cases of small arms ammunition, rolls and rolls of barbed wire, many shells of different calibre and also a safe. We made the mistake of reporting this article to the police, who promptly descended upon us by the bicycle, car and van load. There was much pencil licking and questioning. "Exactly how many feet and inches was it from the dock wall?" "Was the door open or shut?" and, most ludicrous of all, "Did you touch it with your bare hands? We need prints you know." This wasted hours of our precious time, so when another safe was discovered – and a human skull a week later – they remained exactly where they were and went unreported. This was years before police diving units were formed.

We were ordered to search the river bed and a large area around Tower Bridge. This operation took a couple of days and although we found no mines there was clear evidence that a number of explosions had taken place in the river, one directly under the overhead road area of the bridge and a number more too close for comfort, although a careful underwater examination of the towers revealed no damage.

The divers in our party were myself, Jock Gribben (who had been awarded the George Medal for his work in clearing mines from the docks in Holland when diving with a Port Party), and Terry Yetton, who surfaced one day after examining an object with yards and yards of lines hanging from his diving suit. Attached to the lines was a badly damaged parachute and the metal remains of an attachment and plug that had been connected to a massive and very dangerous bomb, the deadly German 'George'. We were pleased that it had exploded underwater.

Jock Gribben had been promoted to Petty Officer and while we were celebrating with a few drinks in a dockside pub we were approached by a couple of well-dressed men who, after getting into our company and buying us a number of drinks, stated that they had observed us while we were working in the docks did we want to make a lot of money? They would supply a cylinder that could be attached to the bilge keel of the ferries that crossed the channel into Dover. This would be used to smuggle goods and could be attached or removed by frogman at night on either side of the Channel. We agreed to meet them again, knowing full well that the following morning we were to leave London and head north. The incident was then reported to HM Customs.

Our diving boat and living quarters was a converted wooden trawler, HMS *Dipper* and one day, in need of a rest from our work, we sailed up the Thames, proudly flying our White Ensign, to be greeted by the opening of Tower Bridge, a surprising event given that the bridge was many feet above our tallest mast and therefore there was no need to open it for use. We came to attention and our captain, Lieutenant John Crawford saluted the gesture. We felt very proud of this chivalrous action of the bridge operators towards us and presumed they were saluting us in return.

After completing our work in London, we sailed into the English Channel and north to Liverpool to commence another dock and harbour search. The job was very much a mirror image of our London search and also bales and bales of crude rubber with a great deal of American war material and rubbish, dropped and dumped from the old days of sailing ships, especially great sodden bales of cotton which we counted in their dozens. It made me think that before cranes, nearly everything when loading and unloading a ship was carried on the backs of stevedores, many of them Chinese sailors who had jumped ships for decades and settled down and raised families in Liverpool.

The city and dock area had taken a tremendous pounding from the air-raids and we found a number of unexploded bombs and two Type C magnetic mines. Although visibility was not too good we could just make out the make and serial numbers on the casings. We also discovered and dealt with a horned mine that had drifted ashore onto the beach at West Kirby – by removing the top plate and setting fire to the explosive inside. I believe that the empty rusting casing stood on the beach for many, many years before succumbing to the drifting sands.

While in Liverpool, Petty Officer Gribben and I were sent to Loch Foyle in Northern Ireland to dive beneath and examine a German type 22 U-Boat that had been moved from an anchorage somewhere in Scotland, where it had laid since the end of the war. We found nothing of danger or interest except, while searching inboard in a locker beneath the conning tower, I found a grey leather officer's jacket, which I gave to my brother, who worked in Preston docks. David stated that he wore it for many winters.

Jock and I enjoyed a couple of nights in Londonderry sampling the Irish Porter (dark-brown bitter beer, like stout but weaker, brewed from charred malt). We entered a pub just underneath the city walls, the only occupants were a couple of men at the, bar, one of very small build similar to a jockey but his companion was a tall broad shouldered person with a very strong physique. I ordered two half pints of porter and the barman slid them over towards me but to my amazement the big man reached over my shoulder, picked up one of the glasses and, in almost one movement and one gulp, drank the contents. I sensed trouble but kept calm and ordered another half pint. I heard Jock Gribben loudly say, "come on Baron, let's get out of here" as the giant made a grab for my second glass, but before he could lift it to his lips I raised my arms in protest and cried with venom "F*** Off mate!" My right arm smashed the glass into his face and he staggered backwards, falling over a table and bashing his head with a sickening thud against a wall. We did not need to count to ten to establish that he was out cold.

"You had better get out of here quick," the barman said. "You have just knocked out Jack Doyle,[12] the heavyweight champion of Great Britain!" (We left rapidly and, needless to say, never returned to that bar again).

Our good old ship HMS *Dipper* was coming to the end of her days and we were ordered to return to Portsmouth where we would commission another ship, an ex-German salvage vessel, which had been renamed HMS *Diver*. We all loved her; she had been built with a gantry crane over her stern, which was perfect for lifting objects (i.e. bombs, mines, torpedoes, etc) from the seabed. She did not have a spoked wheel, like all other ships I had seen or steered, but two buttons, port and starboard, that connected electrically to the rudder. I never got used to it. When underway a ship is alive and you feel it in the wheel.

---

[12] Nicknamed 'The Gorgeous Gael' for his film star good looks, Jack Doyle was never British Heavyweight Champion; he lost his only title fight to Welshman Jack Petersen in 1933, in front of a crowd of 70,000 at London's White City Stadium. The former British Army boxing champion had turned professional just a year earlier and won a string of bouts, making him a hero in his native Ireland. In later years he became an alcoholic and died a pauper in 1978, aged 55.

All ships used by the Underwater Working Party were also crewed by them, except for the engine room staff.

During our period in Liverpool, a warrant officer had joined the ship, a Mr Lieper, who had been in the Royal Navy for many years and had been promoted from the lower deck. His home was in Robin Hood's Bay on the Yorkshire North Sea coast and he spoke often of his knowledge of navigation. The captain ordered him to set a course to Portsmouth but he made a cock-up and we were almost in Weymouth before the mistake was spotted. His excuse was that it was night and the weather and visibility were bad. From then on he was referred to as "Vasco de Lieper" after the famous Portuguese navigator Vasco de Gama. Some months later, however, we all had to bite our tongues and apologize when it was discovered that the compass had not been swung correctly and was a few points out of true. Nevertheless, he still retained his nickname.

For the following two months we were based at the Royal Marine barracks at Eastney, Portsmouth, where we went through a very intensive refresher course in underwater mine and bomb disposal work. We learnt that the only way to dispose of bombs and mines that could not be rendered safe was to detonate them if that could be done safely. Of course, I was already well aware of this from many previous experiences with Commander Crabb.

During our stay at Eastney Barracks we came under the command of a marine sergeant SBS who was determined to toughen us up. He demanded and got complete attention from all the party, including many officers who had joined our party for the exercise and even now I can still hear that instructor's voice bellowing expletives as we staggered along many miles of beach, slithering through waist-deep mud and then hours and hours of swimming, especially in rough weather, dressed in our frogman suits and fins. The SBS sergeant insisted that we should experience long drops and we were taken to a flooded dry dock in Portsmouth, where we were hoisted two at a time by a giant crane up to 50ft and then, on command, plunged feet-first into the water below. Before my first drop I felt nervous and dubious of its benefit but before the training course was over I had managed six drops and was enjoying the exercise. It convinced me that anything was possible, although on my last plunge I was a little careless and finished up with a very sore bum, which lasted for many days.

One morning Terry Yetton and I had swum and floated into the beach on high and roaring surf when we were spotted by a man who was fishing from the shore. Thinking we were in trouble and required assistance, and without a moment's hesitation, he ran, neck-high and fully-dressed into the cold sea, shouting, "Hang on, I will save you!"

When he discovered that we were two frogmen on a training exercise, a mass of expletives and seawater flooded from his mouth and chattering teeth. Very embarrassed, we thanked him for his very brave action.

We were ordered to the Channel Islands on mine clearance with another new boss, Lieutenant Commander "Jackie" Warner, DSC OBE, an ex submarine captain and a man who I grew to admire due to the very civil way he treated the men in our party. He had many long conversations with me, especially about my exploits with Commander Crabb.

When examining the beaches we found a very large reinforced concrete bunker about the size of a house and inside discovered a safe as large as a wardrobe. We were too 'war wise' to check if the door was locked or not, for years of work in this kind of situation had made me extremely wary of booby traps. Commander Warner packed plastic explosive around the handle and locking area, inserted a detonator attached to about one hundred yards of safety fuse, ignited the fuse and we watched its smoke rising as it burned its way rapidly towards the safe. A few moments later we all dived for cover as a massive explosion took place and great chunks of concrete tore into the air and along the beach. Raising our heads we discovered the massive bunker had completely disappeared.

"Have you ever seen anything like that Knowles?" asked 'Jackie' Warner.

"Yes sir," I answered, "but it was a brothel in Leghorn!"

Our next clearance job on Alderney, Channel Isles was to defuze Teller mines that the German occupiers had laid along the beaches to repulse any attempt by the British to retake the island. Our orders were to remove and pile about half a dozen at a time on the beaches, above high water mark, and then detonate them. The resulting explosions carried on day after day and echoed throughout the island and this situation was not satisfactory to the islanders, most of whom were working in the miles of greenhouses there and were afraid that we may crack the glass. A more satisfactory result had to be found and it was suggested that we blow them up underwater at high tide to lessen the effect of the continuous explosions. This we did, but with disastrous results, for the combined effect of these explosions and the increased water pressure they created caused a 'domino effect' as line after line of mines blew up. The German engineers had wired them into a massive booby trap. The ground shook and jolted under our feet and the sand on the beach rippled and waved as though it was water. As the explosions ceased we could plainly hear the crash and tinkling of broken glass as the many nearby greenhouses collapsed.

Fortunately, no one was seriously injured.

We never heard the official outcome of this cock-up but some forty years later I was having lunch in a restaurant near Milan in northern Italy when a gentleman, hearing my wife and I speaking English, asked where we came from. He told us that he was a native of Alderney in the Channel Islands. When I spoke of the German mines he said his grandfather had told him of this incident when he was a little boy. He was amazed that we had met and said that he would be able to dine out on this story for some time to come.

The Admiralty then received a most unusual request from the Government – could they supply a diver to recover a very valuable diamond-tipped drill, which was being used to drill for water for a power station at Fiddlers Ferry on the A1 in Yorkshire. Our party was dispatched north by L.M.S steam train to investigate. When we arrived we were taken to a derrick above a hole containing a pipe 24inches in diameter, which was gushing torrents of brown muddy water to about head height. The site manager explained that the drill tip had been torn off and was now lying at the bottom of the shaft some 60 feet below. Lieutenant Commander 'Jackie' Warner nonchalantly said, "Well men, who goes first?"

I may have been thought of as reckless and impetuous but I loved a challenge and was the smallest member of our team. I looked at the job with some trepidation but volunteered and got dressed in my green frogman suit – the "Pee Cock". Wearing a special type of breathing apparatus that supplied a gas mixture from bottles placed in front of me, which better enabled me to squeeze into the pipe, I made my descent in complete darkness and with great difficulty due to the power of water gushing upwards past my body. We had rigged up a very heavy shot rope, which I grasped and used to heave myself down, hand-over-hand, head-first until, at 45 feet down, the pipe entered a cavern which opened out into a large space about 10 feet wide and some twenty feet high, the bottom of which was covered in stones and boulders that had collapsed from above and from around the sides. In darkness I swam and groped around the area and sensed that it was too dangerous to examine more. Under this lay the drill. Many of the boulders were very large and impossible to be removed and those in the roof of the cavern were loose, so I signalled on my safety line with four tugs that I was ascending. In the complete darkness of the cavern I could feel the water pressure dragging me in the direction of the pipe, and on entering it I was suddenly accelerated upwards towards the surface under great pressure, again head-first, bursting out of the steel tube like a cork from a bottle and landing on my knees and chest with my oxygen bottles clanging beside me. I was not badly injured but the sudden violent change in pressure unfortunately resulted in my left eardrum bursting.

After dressing into uniform and with blood pouring from my ear and my head encased in a towel I was accompanied by Lieutenant Commander Warner to the bus stop, where we caught the bus to the nearest hospital. (Yes, we did go by bus!). This situation would never occur today. While at the hospital a newspaper reporter arrived and that evening the incident was reported in the *Yorkshire Post.*

I was unable to return to diving for three months until the wound had scabbed over.

I don't think the drill bit was ever recovered.

In the early hours of 12th January 1950, at our base at HMS *Lochinvar* in South Queensferry, our diving team was awakened to be informed that the Royal Navy signal 'Sub-Smash' had been received and that we would be flown to the Thames Estuary, where the submarine HMS *Truculent* had been sunk in a collision with the Swedish ship *Divina* seventeen miles north-west of Margate, off the Essex coast.

In London at ten o'clock the same morning, Commander Crabb turned on his radio and heard a public announcement of the collision and a report that a Dutch steamer, the *Almdijk,* had picked up five survivors and two dead men. A later count revealed that fifteen men had been saved aboard the *Divina* but that left over fifty still missing with the *Truculent* lying on the bottom, almost seventy feet below.

We, the clearance diving team, were still waiting for a plane from the RAF to take us down to an airfield as near as possible to the sunken submarine when the signal came for us to stand down. It was later revealed that, tragically, the plane, a Lancaster, had crashed on take-off, killing all the crew. We all counted our blessings.

Commander Crabb, meanwhile, had been in contact with the Admiralty and volunteered his services, along with another diver, Lieutenant Commander Jim Hodges.

Before midnight that same day their offer had been accepted, so they drove the 50-mile journey to Sheerness, only to find when they eventually arrived that no one knew the position of the submarine's distress buoy. The captain of the *Divina* could give no information but later a rescue vessel picked up the buoy.

By now it was becoming light and the only motor boat available was filled with reporters and photographers, who refused to get out until the assistant harbour master came and cleared the boat. They then sped out to a frigate anchored near the buoy, aboard which were some of the survivors. Only after having spoken to them did they learn that there may still be men alive on the submarine in an area beneath the conning tower.

The divers, dressed in rubber suits and wearing fins, with gas mixture bottles on their backs, prepared to dive. The tide had slackened to a knot and a half, previously it had been running at three knots. Hodges went down a heavy weighted shot rope and Crabb dived down the anchor chain of the frigate. They reached the sunken submarine and tapped on the hull, but there was no response. After numerous dives and tapping on the metal coffin there was still no response.

The submarine's escape hatch was twisted and was impossible to open, and their attempt to establish if there were still men aboard had failed. It was only later, when the submarine was raised and towed into Sheerness dockyard, that 10 bodies were discovered. It was believed that the other missing men had escaped but were swept out to sea on the outgoing tide and had drowned. When I later spoke to Commander Crabb he told me that at the time he could have cried with frustration, because he had strongly felt there had been more men aboard.

In the spring of 1950 our Royal Navy clearance-diving team set off on a training exercise to search for the *Florencia*, a galleon from the Spanish Armada, which had been lying under the sand and silt in the Bay of Tobermory on the Isle of Mull since 1588 and which by law was the property of the Duke of Argyle.

We left Portsmouth on the old LMS line, heading north to Scotland by steam-train. This became our fastest and most common mode of transport, resulting in us earning the nickname of 'the British Railway team'. During the journey I left my compartment to visit the toilet and, glancing into another compartment, saw a Naval Officer sitting there with three gold stripes on his sleeve. I was overjoyed to see it was my old boss and diving companion Commander Crabb, who I had last said goodbye to in Venice five years before.

I knocked on his door and recognition dawned in his eyes.

"Hello Sir," I said.

"Hello Knowles," he replied warmly.

What a touching reunion, but we both understood its significance. With him was Commander Rea Parkinson. They were to be the officers in charge of the search and exercise.

At Tobermory our party dived to the bed of the bay, between 80 to 100 feet deep, but our target the galleon still lay another 20 to 30 feet under four hundred years of sand and silt. We searched with pressure probes, trying to locate timber, which we finally found after many days of frustration. In 57 days we spent only 17 underwater due to wind and weather. I found a Spanish dagger sheath and planks of African oak; we also discovered a skull and a good number of human bones, which were sent to Glasgow University but, remembering what had happened in London we did not inform the Police – we thought they may have a problem finding 400-year-old fingerprints anyway.

The exercise had proved lengthy and frustrating and we could stay no longer, but before we left I was privileged to arrange dives for four students who had formed the Amphibians Club, Aberdeen, the first sports diving group in Britain. I personally took charge of the founder and secretary of the club, a Mr Ivor Howitt, and after brief instructions let him dive to the bottom of the bay. I admired these young men greatly, for they had not been trained to dive but they were adventurers with a belly full of guts and searching my memory I cannot recall any other civilians of such calibre in those days, for all of the breathing apparatus they used was home-made. Before we left Tobermory I asked my officers if it would be possible to present them with any of our spare diving gear. I sincerely hope that we found something for them.

We were recalled to HMS *Lochinvar,* our shore base at Port Edgar, almost beneath the Forth Bridge in South Queensferry. The shortest route back from Lochinvar was to Oban and through Loch Ness, the Caledonian Canal and the Moray Firth into the North Sea. Sailing on the Loch was a chance that we could not miss and every diver took a dip to round about fifty feet just to be able to say 'I have dived Loch Ness'. All I recall was that the visibility was almost nil and the water bitterly cold – and we saw no sign of 'Nessy'.

Our new base was established for Royal Navy volunteer divers to train for mine and bomb clearance. Lieutenant Commander Gordon Gutteridge was working in the laboratory on underwater detection aboard HMS *Gossamer* and I had some very interesting conversations with him while he spent many hours in the process of building himself a sports car out of tubular aluminium in an old boatshed. The reason for my interest was that my uncle Jack Hughlock back in Preston was also building his own sports car in a similar fashion, using the same materials. Although Gutteridge had never dived with either Commander Crabb or me during the war, he was very interested to hear of our exploits in Gibraltar, Italy and France. I never saw Gutteridge dive, nor to my knowledge was he a trained Royal Navy clearance diver.

There were also a number of drills being carried out with reference to diving and I took part in a program called the Underwater Vision Experiments (UVE) at the Royal Navy Rosyth dockyard swimming baths and out in the river beneath the Forth Bridge. The idea was put to the Admiralty that by replacing the human retina with that of a cormorant, a frogman would have better vision underwater. As well as myself the group consisted of Lieutenant Commander Hodges, who was a camera expert, Lieutenant Commander Warner, Able Seaman Yetton and a civilian, Mr Joseph Brooks, who I later found to be a naval officer although in all the months of the experiments I never saw him in uniform. I later learned that he was a 'specialist' from HMS *Vernon*.

I volunteered to be the guinea pig, but only on one eye, in case the experiment did not work. In fact, this experiment was called off, but another idea was for me to test a double contact lens where the outer lens protruded a good inch out from the eye, making me look very much like a creature from outer space. These did work, the visibility was amazing and I enjoyed wearing them, although initially they were painful to insert. This may seem like the stuff of James Bond but you must remember this was when frogman diving was in its infancy.

We also took part in experimental dives breathing a mixture of oxygen, helium and nitrogen gases, designed to allow a diver to stay longer underwater.

Many of these experimental dives took place just off the coast of Cornwall and our favourite anchorage at the weekend was in the river at Fowey. One Sunday morning we were hailed by a large yacht requesting permission to tie up alongside us. Commander Warner gave the all clear and invited the people to his cabin for a drink. The two men and two women accepted but while passing over our ship's guard rail one of the ladies gave a cry of dismay, "I've dropped my engagement ring!"

We were moored fore and aft, so I assured her that we could retrieve her precious ring and the whole party got a surprise when informed that they were aboard a diving vessel. One of the gentlemen introduced himself to us as Lieutenant General Brownie and his wife Daphne. I prepared to dive and while entering the water I noticed a hired rowing boat a few yards from the ship's side; in it were two teenage girls who were showing great excitement and interest in the proceedings.

I descended onto a clear sandy bottom at about twenty feet and had hardly searched a yard when I spotted two large diamonds winking at me in a shaft of sunlight. I slipped the ring onto my finger for safety and then prepared to ascend but, glancing above me I saw the rowing boat containing the two girls had overturned. One of them hung onto the gunwale of the boat and was quite safe, but the other girl was sinking down towards me, her colourful cotton summer frock floating up onto her face. She was obviously going to drown if I did not get to her quickly and I swam rapidly upwards towards her.

As soon as she saw me she immediately gathered her frock around and between her legs and the fact that even though she could have easily drowned but was still prepared to display such modesty amazed me! After the girls were rescued I questioned the one that I had saved about her action of modesty and got the very short answer, "My mother always said to watch the sailors!"

Over many years of reading books, watching television and picking up snippets of information, I have become convinced that the lady whose engagement ring I recovered was the famous authoress Daphne Du Maurier, from whom my reward was a kiss on both cheeks.

Our base at HMS *Lochinvar* was very close to the village of South Queensferry and Kirklisten, where the famous liqueur Drambuie was distilled; a distillery had been there since 1795. One evening while out walking along the dockside I heard the sound of a fire engine and saw a plume of smoke rising from the distillery nearby, together with a strong and unmistakable smell of whisky and, to my amazement, whisky started to flow from the drains of the village into the river. Along with other divers and navy personnel I dashed for any container that would hold the golden liquid: HP and tomato sauce bottles were emptied and rapidly washed out, cups, bowls and any available container were sought to hold the precious stuff. In the base that evening, there was much rejoicing and merrymaking but, anticipating a raid by HM Customs and Excise, a couple of my diving companions dropped a number of bottles over the end of the jetty in 20 feet of water, to be retrieved later.

There was indeed a raid the following day by the Customs and Excise men and any bottles found were confiscated and whisky found in any other containers was emptied onto the ground. With much moaning from the watching sailors, a Chief Petty Officer patrolled our quarters in surprise searches, sniffing like a bloodhound. The bottles jettisoned at the end of the jetty could be there to this day; I think a 50 year old Drambuie would be worth diving for.

In 2007 I had a surprise visit to my home in Spain from a group of Clearance Divers from HMS *Grimsby*, led by Coxswain Petty Officer diver Dickman, and we spent a very nice evening together. These were men after my own heart and calibre. A bottle of Pusser's Rum was piped in and many diving stories were exchanged, including the above whisky escapade. I don't know if they have had the opportunity to go and look for it yet or if they ever will?

They were enthralled by my stories of Commander Crabb and I and told me that we were legends in Royal Navy diving circles. They even presented me with the ship's emblem, which I was very proud to receive and have proudly on display in my home.

To my delight, in October 1953 I was ordered – along with Terry Yetton and 'Jock' Frazer and under the command of Lieutenant Commander 'Jackie' Warner – to return to Gibraltar as soon as possible because the SS *Bedenham*, an ammunition ship, had blown up in the harbour. We were informed that the new aircraft carrier HMS *Eagle* was about to leave Portsmouth for sea-trials in the Mediterranean and we were ordered to join her and take passage to Gibraltar. We were also to take with us some new oxygen equipment and diving suits that the Navy wanted us to test out under mine disposal conditions, for our task was to collect thousands of rounds of unexploded ammunition of various calibres that was strewn on the bed of the harbour, as well as numerous bombs which thankfully had not exploded.

On arrival in Gibraltar we commenced our work recovering unexploded shells, boxes of bullets and many other dangerous objects. During this period Terry and Jock were obliged to wear the Salvus diving gear that we were to test but it proved so uncomfortable that we immediately christened it "Clammy Death". Fortunately I had also taken with me my full Italian frogman gear, which enabled me to swim around like a fish whilst they crawled along like crabs on the bottom. The job took several weeks, which allowed me to visit Spain (but this time officially!).

Another interesting event occurred while we were there; we became film extras, playing enemy frogmen in the film *Apes of the Rock* staring George Cole, who was later to become famous for his role as Arthur Daley in the TV series *Minder.* We asked that our "acting" fee be paid into the Royal Navy Benevolent Fund.

As an experienced clearance diver I helped to train and prepare a group who went on to form the Mediterranean Clearance Diving Team, to be based in Malta.

Back at our Lochinvar shore-base, the unit was told to stand by for the return to Britain of a grand old battleship, HMS *Royal Sovereign* (nicknamed 'The Tiddly Quid'). She had been loaned to the Russian navy in 1940 and renamed *Archangel* but never went into action. She made a wonderful sight sailing under the massive Forth Bridge. A skeleton crew had sailed her from Murmansk and as soon as she was anchored they boarded her accompanying Soviet destroyer and sailed away back to Russia.

She lay at anchor for forty-eight hours then we were ordered to examine every square inch of her bottom, rudder and propellers to make sure that no explosive objects had been placed on her. Finding the underwater area all clear we went aboard the now deserted ship to continue searching, where to our absolute disgust we discovered that some members of the Russian crew had defecated on all the mess-deck tables and in the passageways; the sight and smell was disgusting. (This was to play a very important part in what could have been a life-saving decision in my future.) What a disgusting way to say thanks to the Royal Navy and the hundreds of sailors who had died on the terrible Russian convoys that had sailed in appalling conditions for over four years from Britain to Murmansk in an effort to get war materials and food to their struggling country.

My time in the Royal Navy was drawing to a close and I took the offer of a civilian diving job in Canada for a small company called Cansur, working on the St Lawrence River Project. I took a ship out of Liverpool bound for Toronto. This was purely a spring and summer job, due to very unfavourable harsh winter conditions of icebound rivers and lakes. Most of my work involved the inspection of various jetty pilings and taking geological samples from the river and lake beds.

In the early part of winter, when the river had begun to ice over, many freighters battled through the frozen obstruction of ice in an effort to reach port to load or unload before being locked in all through the winter months and this resulted in many of the ships damaging propellers. This called for me to smash thick ice in order to make a bitterly cold and rapid dive of inspection and on one occasion when diving from a jetty to examine a ship's propeller my suit was badly torn when I brushed against a length of steel wire that was attached to a jetty piling which lay underwater. I was dressed in the very familiar Seibe Gorman diving suit with copper helmet and as the freezing water rushed over my body it felt like a hundred needles penetrating me. I was in phone contact with my attendant up above on the jetty who immediately increased the air pressure in my helmet and proceeded to heave me to the surface. I received no injury in the accident but as the winter increased the only ships able to use the river were the specially built icebreakers.

The winter eventually put an end to my work, which I regretted, for the money was good, so reluctantly I had to return home to England.

With the money I had earned and my navy severance pay I bought an old ERF lorry and, having procured a contract from the Star paper mill in Blackburn, I delivered great rolls of newsprint to Fleet Street in London. This was long before motorways and a run from Blackburn to London could take at least ten hours. The conditions I drove under in the early 1950s were quite primitive compared with today's haulage – for example, heaters in cabs were unheard of and in winter I had to cover my legs with sacks to keep warm. There were no rescue services to assist us but other drivers would always lend a hand to change a wheel, etc. In those days wagon drivers were true 'Knights of the Road'.

During this time I was still in regular contact with Commander Crabb, often visiting him on my regular trips to London at his flat in Hans Road. In the spring of 1954 he informed me that the XI Duke of Argyll had asked him to form a civilian diving team in another attempt to find the galleon and its treasure in Tobermory Bay and asked if I would join him. I agreed immediately and we very soon got together a group who had dived on the previous Royal Navy attempt, all of whom had now left the service and were looking for work and adventure.

The galleon had fled around the north tip of Scotland after the defeat of the Spanish Armada in 1588. She was badly damaged and was being refitted in Tobermory harbour by MacLean of Duart (Scotland was, at that time, a neutral country). I was told by the XI Duke that the story was that an emissary of MacLean went on board to demand settlement of the refit but was seized and confined near the ship's magazine. Rather than let the Spanish sail without paying his master, the brave man managed to lay a trail of gunpowder into the magazine and blew up the ship – along with himself.

My first job was to go to Bowling-on-the-Clyde, near Glasgow, where the Duke had purchased an old coastal steamer, the *Ardchattan,* which was waiting to be broken up, the intention being to use her for accommodation and as our dive boat. A retired whaling captain by the name of Lucsmore was to be her skipper and my wife Joan the ship's cook. He was a man who liked his whisky and whenever we would jocularly shout "where away skipper?" he would always reply "South Georgia and there she blows!"

The Author, diving at Tobermory.

We sailed down the Clyde and turned north to the Isle of Mull. In August we started diving, working in shifts eighty to a hundred feet below the surface of the bay, controlling an airlift that functioned like a giant vacuum-cleaner, sucking sand, clay and stones from the seabed. We were hampered by the amount of rubbish that had accumulated in the area over the wreck in four hundred years since she had sunk –

directly in line with the flow of water that roared over a large waterfall nearby.

It fell to me to discover how dangerous our work had become. I was working eighty seven feet below the surface in a deep hole, facing a solid wall of clay, when a boulder slid from the wall behind me and held my body and hard hat copper diving helmet down on the seabed. I was buried and held down for well over an hour while Terry Yetton, my stand-by diver, was sent down, accompanied by Commander Crabb, who had plunged down in his frogman suit. Together they struggled to remove the boulder from my back and drag me clear out of the clay. I was not injured but spent a long, long time hanging onto the shot rope at various depths from the surface doing my decompression stops to ensure that I would not get the dreaded bends.

The Author and Commander Crabb, Tobermory.

Later the following day the Duke and Duchess of Argyle and young Ian, the Marquis of Lorne, came down to our dive boat. They had heard about my accident and were concerned for my wellbeing. Imagine their surprise when they were told that I was down on the seabed again, busily at work. My wife Joan was shocked to learn of my near death experience for I had not informed her of what had happed.

The Author and Commander Crabb, Tobermory.

The Duke and the Marquis of Lorne became regular visitors to our dive site and the Duke took many a "wee dram" with us at the Mishnish and Western Isles Hotels. One evening the famous actress Margaret Rutherford joined our group. She was working for BBC Radio and had come to interview our diving team about our work. She was a very motherly, lively and interesting lady and we all fell in love with her.

On another occasion I was invited to dine with the May family, the other half of the famous Bryant & May match manufactures, who owned a holiday home on Calf Island situated at the entrance of Tobermory bay. A week before the dinner I turned up with a hare that I had snared. There were several children at the house who were very curious at the sight of the creature and who, on hearing that I was a diver, wanted me to tell them stories of what it was like down on the seabed and if I had ever seen monsters down below. I amused them with outlandish stories of how I spoke to the fishes that I met and how I shook hands with a lobster.

The Author preparing colleague Ivor Howitt for a dive.

We worked on for weeks, still removing boulders and clay, for we found that after every storm the area we had just cleared would once again be covered by the tremendous amount of debris washed down from the waterfall. It was a hopeless task and with winter and the bad Scottish weather approaching we felt that our attempt to reach the galleon was well and truly over. I was not sorry to abandon the site for our rewards were very, very poor. Each diver was paid £10 pounds per week plus a loaf of bread, which we thought was a quaint Scottish practice. Also, we were informed that we could claim one percent of any treasure that we found, so it was evident that we were diving for the adventure rather than the money. Many of the good people of Tobermory laughed when we enquired about the loaf of bread and told them the amount of our wages. "The Inverary Argyles are noted for their clenched fist," they said.

The Author, Tobermory.

On the day we were due to leave Tobermory, Commander Crabb and I dived to clear a trawler's screw, which was fouled by a tangle of wire. We had great difficulty when the trawler's anchor dragged and we drifted amongst the wire towards some vicious rocks. We surfaced and clambered aboard and an hour later, with the trawler firmly re- anchored, we went back over the side and finished the job.

"A near do that was, Sir," I said.

"Yes Knowles," he replied, with his snorting laugh. "Another ten minutes' hell!"

We both grinned, for we had been using these expressions for the last eleven years in time of trouble.

During our period of diving with the Royal Navy and for the Duke of Argyle we were amazed at the number of requests for help that we got from trawlers and other vessels to clear ropes and wires that had become entangled around the ships' propellers and to clear blocked inlet pipes. An idea and opportunity arose that we could form a diving and engineering company on one of the Shetland Isles very near to the fishing grounds, thus saving any fishing vessel a long journey to the home ports of Aberdeen or Fleetwood for repairs. The Commander and I discussed this scheme for many hours and it was decided that he would try to obtain financial backing. A few days later our group broke up, with great disappointment at not finding any treasure.

Diving vessel moored in front of Western Isles Hotel.

We left Scotland and I returned to my haulage business and the hour-after-hour crawl, usually in thick fog, from Blackburn to London, loaded with rolls of newsprint, through the twisting country roads of those days. I was to experience what future travel and trucking would be like when I drove on the very first stretch of motorway in Great Britain that had been built, the Preston by-pass, which ran a few miles north and south of the river Ribble. It was amazing; I found it straight and wide with a clean unruffled surface which gave my old lorry added speed and comfort and it was with dismay that all too soon I found myself back onto roads that the Roman Legions had marched over and upon which stagecoaches had rumbled.

Where the motorway junction entered Preston at the river Ribble was a truck stop with a chip shop, café and sweet shop. This sweet shop, back in the 1920s and 30s, had been owned by my grandmother. In those days it only opened in summer, selling pots of tea, cakes and ice cream for families who would go down to the river at weekends to sit on the sandy banks and swim. All this has now gone, to be replaced by a very nice and well known hotel called The Tickled Trout.

In my childhood days of the 1920s the banks of the river Ribble would be crowded with families every weekend in summer, enjoying picnics and children paddling in an area of the north bank called Sandy Bottom – the warm and shallow water near to the Half Penny Bridge that spans the river and leads into Preston.

In those days my biggest thrill was to spend a day at Blackpool – which cost one shilling return by steam train from Preston – and maybe win the penny that my parents offered if I spotted the famous tower before they did. I always hoped that the tide was out so that I could play on the miles of wonderful clean sand that the resort boasted.

I recall that the annual holiday was always the second week in August for the Working Class people of Preston and that it was a holiday without pay. My father's wage as a Plate Layer for the LMS (London Midland & Scottish Railway) was two pounds, two shillings per week, so my Mother used to save a shilling and a few coppers every pay day for the next holiday. Holidays abroad were just a distant dream in those days.

If my memory serves me right, children were not as demanding in my younger days. I know that my Friday penny went a long way further than maybe a couple of pounds today, but I observe that the children of today seem to be continuously eating and never seem to be content with what they have got and the forever the cry of "Mum, can I have... or I want..." In my opinion a lack of discipline and parental control is to blame, but then again this is the year 2008 – but I still don't condone it.

The Author in the 1950s.

6. A Spying Job in Portsmouth

In October 1955 I was contacted by Commander Crabb and asked if I would like to join him on 'a small job in Portsmouth'. He said that we would get a fair fee, but over the telephone he was reluctant to give more details. I said I would be happy to join him and I met up with him in London, where I was introduced to a Matthew Smith, who was a member of the American CIA and who I christened "GD" because of his annoying habit of prefixing everything and everyone with "God-damned".

I soon discovered, due to his body language and many a slip of the tongue, that he was, or had been, an American naval officer and was here to organize a mission to look under and examine the hull of the Soviet cruiser *Sverdlov*, which was to visit Portsmouth on a goodwill visit and to take part in the Spithead Review. I must admit I was very excited at the prospect of being on a secret service mission. I also must admit that during the exciting clashes with the Italian frogmen in Gibraltar I had often secretly wished that I could have joined them in their clandestine operations, for the prospect of drifting and swimming across "The Bay" to put a mine on an enemy ship would have been a great challenge.

And now, here I was, with the opportunity to prove myself in a similar fashion but without placing a mine!

Although now running a haulage business, I had kept in touch with diving by becoming the Dive Master of Darwen Sub Aqua Club in Lancashire and still felt at home in a watery environment. I left Preston as usual and delivered my cargo of newsprint to Fleet Street and then picked up Commander Crabb at his flat and proceeded to drive down to Portsmouth. We arrived in the late evening; the weather was very overcast with a cold wind. I was now told the purpose of our dive. The American Navy, the CIA and the Admiralty wished to know what made the Russian cruiser *Sverdlov* so very manoeuvrable, displaying a good turn of speed on her entry to Portsmouth. The cruiser was now in British waters, so this covert operation was organized under the umbrella of the CIA.

My wagon became an integral part of the plot, parking it on the seafront and in sight of the distant railway jetty where the *Sverdlov* lay alongside with her accompanying Russian destroyers. Using the wagon tarpaulin as cover, we dressed in our diving gear, which was of Italian origin, and our rebreathers, which we both preferred, for this apparatus did not discharge bubbles that could be spotted by sentries on the ships above. We had kept this Italian diving gear from our wartime exploits, as it was far superior to the British gear for this type of operation. It was a complete eye-opener to me that my old boss had got himself into this den of intrigue but I had always had an unshakable faith in everything that he did and followed him eagerly.

Smith joined us to discuss the plan. In the event of us being captured Commander Crabb suggested that we ask for political asylum. I protested, for I had no intention of spending the rest of my life in a cold country with little personal freedom, poor food and lacking in home comforts. My mind returned to the incident on HMS *Royal Sovereign* (The Tiddly Quid) some years before in the Firth of Forth and the insulting, disgraceful way that the Russian sailors had behaved. I had no wish to serve with that type of people. Commander Crabb, unaware of my thoughts, grinned and just said "I feel very Italian. Let's go!"

It was now very dark and well past midnight. We had estimated that the distance we had to cover meant the operation would take around three to four hours, depending on the current and tide, for our progress by necessity would have to be very slow and cautious. Dressed in our Italian two-piece diving suits, we donned our breathing sets and, after shaking hands with "GD", made a final check that there was no one around to witness our entry into the water. It was at this stage that the reality of the situation made me tremble with anticipation. On our heads we wore skull caps with black netting that hung down over the head and face. This allowed us to see but broke up the silhouettes of our heads when on the surface.

Our approach to the cruiser seemed never ending as our intention was to move at no more than a drifting speed with an occasional gentle kick of our fins, for as we got nearer to our target any splash would be heard. By now I had placed a floating fish box over my head, which would not justify a second glance and afforded me extra cover. We were also obviously required to keep a very careful lookout for any craft that may have been moving in the harbour because we could have been seriously injured or even killed as we dared not call out a warning to any oncoming craft.

We drifted gently around the stern of the destroyers which were vividly ablaze with light and I could make out Quartermasters and sentries on the upper decks, for the Commander and I had decided that the safest way was not to dive under the destroyers to get to our target. On reaching the *Sverdlov* I was amazed at her size; this was my first close up view of her and my mind returned to my Italian frogman friend Petty Officer Vago Giari and the tales he told me about his clandestine operations against us in the Bay of Gibraltar. During the whole of this operation I followed the information he had given me on how he had executed successful attacks on our shipping, for his experience was invaluable and very rare.

I noticed that the Commander had placed a large bunch of seaweed over his head as a disguise. Giving myself a gentle guff of oxygen I sank down to the bilge keel, my entire body was tingling with adrenalin and although the water was freezing cold I felt no discomfort. Soon the Commander joined me and together we swam gently, still maintaining our covert activity to examine the two rudders and the propellers but we found nothing unusual. Touching and giving each other hardly discernible hand signals, we gently kicked our fins and swept our way along the bilge keel towards the bow, where I was to wait until he had searched forward. All around us was almost total blackness, except for a faint light that was penetrating down through the water from the dockside and the destroyers alongside. Once my oxygen bottle clanged against the steel bilge keel, as did the Commander's, but I was not too concerned, for the activity inside the ship, just above our heads, was very noisy with the constant roar of fans and generators from her engine and boiler rooms.

My wait seemed eternal and I knew that my oxygen was getting low and I was about to swim to the bow when, peering through the gloom, I saw the shadowy figure of the Commander approaching me with his thumb stuck up in a gesture of success. He signalled for me to follow and together we moved to where I found myself on the edge of a large circular opening in the bottom of the hull. We went up inside the dark space and examined a propeller that could be lowered and directed to give thrust from the bow and help the ship's manoeuvrings.

We were overjoyed and, still keeping our operation secret, made our long, slow swim back with extreme care to our rendezvous. On our way back, and now swimming side by side against an increasingly strong current, I asked him why he took so long to examine the propeller in the bow. His answer was: "I thought I would just examine the destroyers while we were here, but I found nothing new."

This was the Crabb I knew and loved.

Without changing into our civilian clothes we crawled onto my wagon and under the tarpaulin, where now, cold and a little exhausted, we cracked open a bottle of single malt whisky and reported our findings to "GD Smith", who we found had fallen asleep in the cab. It was almost daybreak but for me the night had gone like a flash. Smith then left – to report to his superiors, I presumed.

Changing back into our normal clothes the Commander and I climbed into the cab and drove the long but now joyous road to London and his flat in Hans Road – a small, one-bedroom, first-floor apartment, which he kept very clean and tidy, in true naval fashion.

Still celebrating, we drank a few more tots of whisky and in a slightly drunken state the Commander bemoaned the fact that the navy had "bowler-hatted" him but somehow to me his moaning did not ring true and I felt that he was trying to fool me, yet tell me something. He then stated that he had plans to join the Canadian or Russian navy.

I was not surprised at his comment re the Russians, for way back in Venice on the island of Le Vignole, the Italian HQ of the Tenth Flotilla, we had both listened with intent to Lieutenant Eugenio Wolk, who had trained the Gamma Group. He was a man of authority, six feet four inches tall and an Olympic swimmer. Many a young Italian frogman in training had felt the weight of his fists. Wolk was a dyed-in-the-wool communist and stated that as soon as possible he would be going to Russia to take up a position in the Soviet naval brigade called *Spetsnaz* – or to give it its full title *Voyska Spetsial Nogo Naznachenniya.* The major role of this brigade was to be concerned with mines and underwater sabotage.[13]

By 1945 the Royal Navy had become the leading force in this field, having gained a great deal of knowledge from the Italians who were, up to then, the world leaders. The Soviet Union was desperate to catch up and was looking outside of Russia for people who would be willing to pass on their expertise in underwater operations. Commander Crabb had casually said to me that joining the *Spetsnaz* would be a good move but this was always when he was feeling low after he had been out looking for a job – especially on one occasion when the only work he was offered, because of his

[13] I later discovered that Lieutenant Eugenio Wolk did not go to Russia but had been accepted in the Argentine Navy to form a swimming attack group similar to the Italian Gruppa Gamma.

stature, was that of a 'sandwich-board man'. I never took his comments seriously for they often did not ring true.

I reminded him of our idea to open a diving and engineering shop on Shetland but he informed me that he could not find the cash or backing. Frankly, I do not think that he had done a thing about it.

With regard to the Canadian offer, it would have meant a demotion to Lieutenant Commander, which I knew he would not be prepared to accept, as this would mean a loss of status.

Often when we were alone the Commander would speak of the early days of his time in the training establishment at HMS *Volcano* and his introduction to mine disposal and the long hours he lay awake thinking of how he would tackle his first mine. During this visit to the flat I spotted a bright metal cylinder lying on the lower shelf of his coffee table on top of a number of typed sheets of paper. It measured approximately 40cm x 5cm.

"What is this metal object?" I called to the Commander, who was in the kitchen.

"Oh! The blip stick. It's something that Taylor and I are working on at the moment," he replied. I furtively and rapidly cast my eye over a little of the writing on a document beneath the cylinder, a list of names included Suez, Kirsch, Istanbul and a number of graphs and fathom readings of the Baltic. I guessed that this was to do with his secret work, but for whom or for what I did not know, although I realized this work with the 'blip stick' was the reason for his frequent disappearances for some considerable time and his secret work for the Special Branch and Naval Intelligence under the command of admiral Mountbatten. Taylor by the way, I discovered through Alistair Malcolm, was some kind of electrical boffin in MI5. I asked my boss about the work he was doing for the Intelligence service and his reply was. "It is politically very near to the bone Knowles. but if you had been commissioned you could have joined me."

That evening, over a number of drinks, Commander Crabb said, "Knowles, do you realize that we have gone through this long war together and done hundreds of dives under ships bottoms, including troop ships with thousands of men aboard, removed many, many mines and only one man died in all our operations. Why did we do it?"

"To beat Hitler, of course," I replied.

"Nonsense," he responded. "We did it for those in peril." He was right, for our work saved not only the ships but thousands of men floating above us.

Many months later and after much prompting I at last received payment for "the *Sverdlov* job" from the Pay Master, who to my surprise was Lieutenant Murray Micklejohn RN, an ex-member of Naval Intelligence who I found out later had worked in Gibraltar during the war. The reward for my night's work came to the princely sum of £40 and no more. I state this because many reporters and writers say that I was paid as much as £600 – just wild and crazy guesswork on their part.

The Russian cruiser 'Sverdlov'.

7. The Disappearance of Commander Crabb (April 1956)

After the *Sverdlov* operation I continued making my regular runs from Preston to Fleet Street, delivering rolls of newsprint, and on most occasions I would visit the Commander. On one of these visits he informed me that an author by the name of Marshall Pugh, a young Scot, was writing a book about him and I and our wartime exploits and would I be willing to assist them in this task? I eagerly agreed, as all the events were fresh in my mind, so together we spent many happy hours reminiscing at Pugh's home. CPO Ralph Thorpe also had appeared to assist.

One evening I arrived at Pugh's to be informed that there was a change of plan. Crabb and Pugh had been intending to go out to a dinner invitation but as Pugh was unable to attend. They suggested that I take his place instead. I agreed and we took a taxi to an address in Tite Street, Chelsea. En route, however, we stopped at the Courtauld Institute to pick up another passenger, who was introduced to me as Mr Blunt, a tall, angular-faced gentleman who appeared to know Crabb very well. On arriving in Tite Street we entered a flat, where there was long, comfortable lounge, four sofas, side tables and, in a corner, a bar. In the centre was a very large table with twelve to fourteen seats.

I was to discover that these meetings were referred to as "The Last Suppers", hence the number of seats. This, I was later to discover, was a very apt name, for while at Cambridge University, Blunt had recruited people with communist leanings for the KGB through a society called "The Apostles".

I was introduced to various groups of people, all drinking heavily and addressing each other as 'comrade'. There were lots of young, intelligent men, obviously homosexual, and most of the conversation revolved around politics, the glories of communism and the Soviet Union. Blunt was seated at the table, surrounded by young men hanging on his every word. They referred to him as "The Queen Mother".

Afterwards, Crabb asked if I had enjoyed the party and I replied, "Frankly Sir, not very much. I enjoyed the booze but the conversation was way over my head."

Crabb, Pugh and I visited the Last Supper meetings a number of times over the next few months and at each visit I got more concerned at the blatant political overtones that were being discussed loudly and the very anti-British comments.

"Have you known Mr Blunt for long"? I asked the Commander one day, while visiting him at his flat.

"Yes," was his reply. "My cousin Kitty worked for him for a considerable time as his PA while he was director of the Courtauld Institute."

Frankly, at that time I was not really interested, nor had any idea where it all was leading. I tackled both companions but they dismissed it with a shrug. A number of times the Commander brought up the subject of him taking up a position with the Soviet *Spetsnaz,* and I began to realise that he had virtually made up his mind to defect. This resulted in he and I having a number of arguments, during which I reminded him of what we had both gone through during the war in our battle against Fascism and the Nazi party. I had always looked up to him as a war hero and a patriot and when I reminded him of this his reply was, "One can be a patriot *and* a communist. Don't forget Knowles, we are not at war with Russia, and during the last war they were our allies."

I shook my head in disbelief, for these words were not coming from the wonderful person I had followed blindly for years and years. He had become a stranger.

I felt that the situation was getting out of hand and made the grave decision to inform the authorities of Crabb's intentions. I wrote a letter to M15, addressed "To Whom It May

Concern" and, as I did so, I felt sick, for I was betraying a man that I loved. Within 48 hours I was contacted by a gentleman who introduced himself has Colonel Alistair Malcolm, who arranged a meeting with me in a bar behind Piccadilly. Malcolm arrived, a slim, middle-aged man with an educated and slight Scottish accent. He instantly put me at ease by saying, "Don't worry, old chap, we know all about the parties. We have someone in there." But he would not enlighten me as to who this person was. I suspected that it was Anthony Blunt, but I could not explain why. He asked me to continue to attend the parties and to keep in touch with him.

I was feeling more and more embarrassed at every Last Supper meeting that I attended, for I felt that I was being ignored and that I had become a sort of mascot, for it became very obvious to me that I was shut off from certain conversations and I felt like a pawn in a game of chess. Amongst a number of men who were introduced to me at the Last Suppers, one name remains in my memory, I think because he was a very quiet person but a giant of a man. This was Howard Dines and his main interest and conversation with me was of my dives with Commander Crabb in Gibraltar, Italy and the South of France. He used to embarrass me by exclaiming loudly, "Oh how brave you both were!" He informed me that he was a manager at an employment exchange in London.

At one of the parties Commander Crabb introduced Pugh and I to Ray Noble, the band leader who wrote *Love Is the Sweetest Thing* and to Labour MP Bernard Floud, who committed suicide in 1967 after being interviewed by M15 about his KGB connections. Also there was also Roger Hollis, future head of M15, whom the Commander greeted like a long-lost friend. Some people have since claimed that Hollis was connected to the Cambridge spy ring.

I recall one occasion when a lady was introduced to me as Lillian Hellman, an American author and a very "dyed in the wool" communist. She was the only female I ever saw at Tite

Street and I had a very long and interesting conversation with her. She informed me that her 'husband' had been arrested under the McCarthy communist witch-hunts and that he had been portrayed as a "Pinko Fag", an American expression that I had never heard before. She said that her husband, or partner, was Dashiell Hammett, the detective-story writer and author of *The Maltese Falcon* and that he was in jail in New York.

"I was asked blatantly," she said, "if I was a communist and I answered by claiming the Fifth Amendment." She was ordered to appear before the Congress House Un-American Activities Committee to admit her political beliefs and to name any suspected Communists that she might know. She informed me that she had been given a London address by a friend and "got the hell out" of the United States.

Another person who introduced himself was a man who approached me and said, "You do not remember me but we worked together on that German U-Boat at Lishali, Loch Foyle in Northern Ireland. I worked inside the boat." This was a reference to a special search I was sent to on a U-Boat that had been towed in from where it had surrendered at the end of the war. He spoke with a lovely Irish brogue and I discovered that his name was Michael Walsh. I also changed my assumption that Blunt was the inside man in favour of Walsh, for I felt that he was a member of MI5 and the person that Colonel Malcolm had alluded to. I asked the Colonel, but was greeted by a burst of laughter as he turned his back on me.

Deep down, I could not accept the fact that Commander Crabb, whom I had held in great esteem for so many years, was about to defect to Russia. There had to be another explanation and my mind raced with thoughts.

Once I asked him, "Is there something that you have not told me Sir?" and after a few moments of silence he gave a nod of his head, grimaced, shrugged his shoulders and replied: "There is no more to be said Knowles, and for God's sake get a grasp." I wondered if he was he being sent in as a double agent, as I hoped, and if so I was starting to feel terribly guilty because of my disclosures to MI5. At a meeting with Alistair Malcolm I told him of my feelings of guilt and he replied, "Sydney, your beloved Commander is doing this for his country, just as you are, so please do not worry about that." He then shut up abruptly. It was obvious that he had said more than he had intended to say and I could drag no more information out of him.

One evening I joined Commander Crabb for a drink and to meet a number of his friends aboard a yacht that had just sailed up the Channel and into the Thames. She had tied up alongside a great number of houseboats at Chelsea and during the evening he received a parcel of oil paintings from one of the three occupants, a middle aged man wearing a fierce red beard. During drinks and conversation I discovered that they had arrived from Lisbon, Portugal where they had been occupied in the opening of a publishing house to be called the Albatross Press. The Commander warned me to keep my face straight when he introduced me to the gentleman with the beard, whose name was Wallace Antonov Costa but who preferred being addressed as 'WC'. I saw the parcel some days later at a Last Supper meeting; it was lying on a table at the rear of the room, close to Anthony Blunt's chair. A week later I was studying a new painting on the wall at the Hans Road flat, depicting a man slumped in a chair, wearing a smart, well-trimmed beard and on his head a tall, shiny, black hat, as worn in the eighteen hundreds. Over his lap was draped a black-stocking'd female leg and on a rug between his feet was a bright, snow-white model of an elephant with its trunk raised into the air, measuring about eighteen inches tall.

"Any comments?" asked the Commander.

"Yes," I said. "I do not understand it Sir," at which he gave a snort, spun round and almost viciously said, in a raised voice, "It's French, Knowles, it's *French!*" and I suspected it was another canvas that had passed through my boss's hands since I first saw him dealing with art when he exchanged a case of American C-rations and tins of Bully Beef with a Catholic priest for a small painting when we were in Siena, Italy in 1944. Unfortunately, I never saw the subject of that painting.

For a long period the question of his proposed move to join *Spetsnaz* seemed to be shelved, although together we visited a couple of Last Suppers, where he spent the majority of the evening in deep conversation with "Queen Mother" Anthony Blunt. This nickname intrigued me; I thought it must be because he seemed to be the "leading light" at these very obviously homosexual gatherings, but I was to discover that the name was in connection with his work as the curator of the Queen Mother's paintings at Clarence House.[14] I was also to discover later that secretly Commander Crabb had accompanied Blunt to Clarence House on a number of occasions, to the Commander's obvious delight, and on a few occasions he had been there when Admiral Mountbatten had been in attendance.

I recall that on at least three occasions in 1943 in Gibraltar Commander Crabb worked for Lord Mountbatten and one day, to the surprise of the whole team, we were visited by Commander Hancock, who informed us to change into number one uniforms for the visit of the Admiral. But after much cleaning of the mess in Jumpers Bastion, hiding Nina the dog and the parrot and being inspected by the Chief Petty Officer, he failed to appear, due to a change of plan and a very important meeting at the Rock Hotel, accompanied on this occasion by a number of men in civilian clothes. Everyone knew about the meetings but nothing of their contents and on each visit my boss would disappear for a few days. A couple of days after a meeting at Tite Street, to which, surprisingly, for some reason I had not been invited, the Commander informed me that "Dickie sends his regards and a well done on the Sverdlov job." I presumed that the

[14] Anthony Blunt was also a third cousin of the Queen Mother.

compliment came from the First Sea Lord, who was in attendance there.

Was the plan to go to Russia Blunt's idea? After all, he was later discovered to be a double agent. Had MI5 discovered this plan? As Malcolm had told me, "We have someone in there Knowles, don't worry old chap." To my mind – and to the rest of the country – it would have been unthinkable that a war hero and a diver who knew so much about the new underwater warfare and tactics – a field in which Britain had become world leaders – would have been allowed to defect.

I was stunned when the Commander then asked me to join him on another "job".

The *Sverdlov's* sister ship, the *Ordzhonikidze,* was about to arrive very soon in Portsmouth on a "goodwill" visit, bringing Premier Nikita Khrushchev and Marshal Nicolai Bulganin to Britain.

"We have been asked to examine her, just as we did with the *Sverdlov.* Of course, you will join me Knowles?" he said.

"No Sir, I cannot." I replied. "My wife is not well and I must return home."

That evening he asked me to come with him to see the film *Marty* – Rod Steiger was his favourite film star – and again he asked me to join him on this next Portsmouth dive. I just could not understand the necessity to go under the *Ordzhonikidze* when our operation under her sister ship the *Sverdlov* had been such a success. What was the point? I had a premonition that this would be a dive too far, and while I had used the excuse that my wife was ill, my real reason was my knowledge of what was happening behind the scenes. I have to say that I hated lying to him.

I was very concerned about the Commander and asked him who he had got to take my place. He told me he had managed to find someone but would not reveal his name, although he did tell me that they had been up to a lake in Wales, near Brecon – where I believe today members of the Special Services are trained – and that their secret test dives together had been satisfactory and with one slip of the tongue I discovered that his new dive buddy was an ex Royal Marine SC1 CC.

I again implored him not to take this 'job', as I still believed there was something wrong.

I again contacted Colonel Malcolm and informed him of Commander Crabb's intention to dive under the *Ordzhonikidze*. He responded by stating, "There is nothing to worry about – we have everything under our control and he will not get away from us." My reaction to this news was, *great, they are going to stop the operation*, but secretly I hoped they would never tell the Commander that it was me who had informed them of his intentions.

The Ordzhonikidze.

"By the way Sydney," said Colonel Malcolm. "You recall the large chap that you spent long periods chatting with at Tite Street? Well, it has been reported to me that he died of a heart attack," and with a chuckle in his voice he continued, "while on holiday in Lisbon, Portugal."

I wondered if he worked for the group who stated that they were forming the publishing house Albatross Press.

I heard no more from either Commander Crabb or Colonel Malcolm, but about ten days later the news was released to the general public that Commander Crabb was missing.

My worst fears had been realised.

I was contacted by the BBC, who wished to interview me and give my view as to what may have happened to the Commander. A time and date was arranged for a visit to a studio on May 4th but only a couple of hours before I was due to go on air a D-Notice was issued upon the proposed broadcast. I returned home very angry. Who were these people who could so easily gag me? This was Great Britain, the land of Free Speech and I thought of all the years of hell that I had gone through in the war to uphold this.

The very same day I was contacted by Preston CID and taken to the central police station, where I was questioned closely for some hours. When did I last speak to him? And if he was found could I identify him? On a sheet of paper I drew the location of any scars that I knew of on the Commander's body. I was also told not to speak to the press. My statement to the police covered three sheets of foolscap in longhand, which I was asked to read and then sign each one if I found them to be correct. On leaving the police station I was surrounded by reporters but had to tell them that the police had instructed me to make no comment. I returned in my old lorry to my home in Preston with a heavy heart and prepared for the following day and another trip with newsprint to Fleet Street.

After unloading in London I decided to drive down to Portsmouth, my intention being, if at all possible, to find out what had happened. I visited a bar where most of the navy lads used to drink and where I knew I could make contact with someone from HMS *Vernon*, the Underwater Countermeasures and Weapons Establishment. I met several officers who I was acquainted with but no-one could enlighten me as to what had occurred. One person did remark, "It's no good looking for him; he's gone. But I can reveal no more."

"Gone where?" I asked, but he did not reply.

I decided to contact Marshall Pugh, only to find that he knew no more than me. I asked him if this had anything to do with the "Last Suppers" but he said that he had no knowledge of what had been going on there. He seemed a little scared and visibly shocked, but said he had rung the secretary of the Deputy Chief of Naval Staff to point out that Commander Crabb had friends in journalism and that the way the affair was being handled would provoke publicity rather than prevent it. Otherwise the only reply from him was that Crabb was missing but might be picked up by a trawler, although this was very unlikely.

I revisited Portsmouth, where a young reporter from the *Daily Mail* asked me if I was prepared to dive in search of the Commander. I of course replied "Yes". So, dressing in full view and with the newspaper's cameraman in attendance, I prepared to dive but inwardly knowing that I had absolutely no chance of finding anything in that great expanse of water. I was approached by a serving naval officer, a Mr Brooks, now in uniform and who I knew very well from our work together in UVE.

"Don't dive," he said. "Crabbie's not there. I know all about this but under the Official Secrets Act I can say no more Knowles. I would hate for any friend of mine or Buster's to be put in danger. I know there is nothing to gain. Don't ask me why, I just do."

I thanked him and abandoned my dive. I drove home devastated; again my worst fears had been realised.

For weeks afterwards the papers were full of speculation as to what had happened to Commander Crabb. Questions were asked in Parliament and Mr Gaitskell, the Leader of the Opposition, said that he would have to conclude that the British or some other country's Secret Service must have been involved. He is the only person I know that made a statement and got anywhere near to the truth of the matter and, as a matter of fact, he had hit the nail on the head, although he had not the slightest idea of what had occurred.

As time went by, I constantly wondered what had become of the Commander. Was he dead? Or, as many people were stating, was he in Russia? Many crazy ideas floated through my head. I honestly and sincerely expected the Commander to contact me and I asked Malcolm if the whole operation was a red herring, for I was beginning to think that it was. But he could give me no more information other than to say "We will have to wait and see old boy".

This was the last time I spoke to Alistair Malcolm, for although I telephoned him again numerous times, the line was always dead.

I was franticly contacted by the commander's girlfriend, Pat Rose, a very smart blonde and good-looking woman who could turn men's heads. She asked me if I knew anything about Crabb's disappearance. I told her no. She was annoyed at me for not going with him, as I had on other occasions, for we had dived together for almost twelve years. Again, I reiterated my excuse that my wife was ill. I met Pat again later when Bernard Hutton asked me to help him with research for his book *Commander Crabb is Alive*.)

In early May, Pat Rose left England to join her brother James and his wife Naomi at their home in the South of France, as she was being continually pursued by journalists.

A fortnight after her arrival, two photos appeared in an East German newspaper, one showing Pat by her brother's swimming pool and another in riding gear, stood between her brother and sister-in-law. As there were only two copies and Pat had one and Commander Crabb the other, this gave Pat the idea that Crabb had defected to Russia and was still alive, but in my opinion Mathew Smith must have obtained these photos when he cleared Crabb's belongings out of the Sally Port Hotel. What benefit this could have been to Smith and his CIA colleagues I do not know, as this only helped to perpetuate the rumours that Crabb was still alive and living in Russia, unless this was a cover for what had really befallen my dear friend and Commander. Pat was also contacted by phone and told that Crabb was alive, but I believe this was all just a hoax perpetuated by J. Bernard Hutton to help promote his book *Commander Crabb is Alive*.

I was also contacted by Mrs Beatrice Crabb, the Commander's mother, who asked me to call on her at her bungalow in a small village in Kent. I was greeted warmly by a small, gentle lady, who said there was no need for formal introductions as she felt she knew me so well, as her son had spoken of me often in his letters, both throughout the war and later in peacetime. She gave me tea and cake and we chatted about Lionel. I told her how all our diving party in Gibraltar felt about him, that he was a father figure to us all and that he was referred to in the Royal Navy as "The Underwater Warrior". She replied to this by raising her voice slightly. "Sydney, he was also a gentleman and my son." She asked if I would like his spare uniform that was hanging in one of her wardrobes. I am now sorry to say that I declined. I did meet her again on a number of occasions but she had changed; grief had had taken its toll and she was not the proud lady I had first met.

Fourteen months later, on June 9th 1957, a body in a rubber suit was discovered by a Mr John Randall while out fishing off Pilsey Island. Along with two of his companions, they hauled the headless and handless body into the boat and took it back to the shore, where the police and RAF from a nearby base took over and the body was transferred to Chichester mortuary.

Dr D.P. King, a pathologist to the Chichester Hospitals Group, spent over an hour examining the remains and prepared a 300-word report for the inquest, which was set for June 11th. In his report he stated that he had examined the body most carefully and could not trace any scars or other marks of identification. Dr King's statement at this time would become relevant in the second inquest, held on June 26th.

I had sold my lorry by this time and was working at a swimming pool as a temporary attendant. Some time before June 11th, two men in civilian clothes and wearing bowler hats, who identified themselves as MI5 officers, informed me that a body in a rubber frogman suit had been found and requested me to go to Chichester to help in an effort to identify it. I decided to ride south on my Vincent Black Shadow motorbike. Upon my head I wore a beret (it was many years before helmets became compulsory) and about 10 miles outside Chichester I was stopped by a police car and another car carrying the two men who had visited me at the swimming pool. They asked me to step into their car, where they said, "We wish to speak to you before you see the body. On arriving at the mortuary you will be met by a Chief Inspector of police and he will have a word with you." I asked if that was the only reason they had stopped me and they then went on to say that as a Navy man, and having signed the Official Secrets Act, they did not wish me to be interviewed by the press. They then produced a document that had *Official Secrets Act* printed at the top; it was written in small print on four or five sheets of paper and this document they asked me to sign, which I declined, for I felt that I was being bullied.

"Well, now go ahead," they said, "and report to the Chief Inspector."

When I arrived at the mortuary, the Chief Inspector took me inside to view the body. One other person was present, a gentleman in a white coat, who the Inspector asked to leave. I was shocked when the Inspector, holding a handkerchief over his mouth and nose, removed a sheet from a headless body, wearing a battered and faded green rubber frogman suit that I recognised immediately. It had been cut by the pathologist (I presume by the order of the coroner) from the neck area down the entire body, past the genitals and down to the feet on both sides and through the shoes, revealing very well-preserved feet. It was with some distaste that I examined the body; it was giving off a stench, although not like or as strong as the corpse I had handled in the river Arno at Florence. All the flesh was as white as lard and I saw that the pubic hair was very dark; the skin had the blubbery appearance of tripe.

My natural instinct was to examine behind the left knee for an inverted Y scar that I knew existed, being the result of the injury he had incurred in the harbour of Leghorn. As I had personally dressed this wound and seen the resulting scar many times, I knew exactly what I was looking for. I also knew of a very pronounced scar on the left thigh, caused by a seawater boil, something that affected some divers after long hours immersed in seawater without a suit. I found no scars at all.

I examined the remains of the body carefully and realised that this was not the body of Commander Crabb, but I did identify the faded green frogman diving suit as one being of a type issued to the Royal Navy and christened by divers "The Pee Cock" because in the genital area a non-magnetic metal plug had been fitted so that the diver, when out of the water, could easily unscrew it to urinate, cutting out the problem of undressing and redressing with the help of an attendant. Also, on the upper and shoulder area, there were the rotted and faded remains of a white diving or submariner's heavy duty sweater.

I turned to the Inspector and stated, "This is not the body of Commander Crabb."

We retired to an adjoining office where we were met again by the MI5 people.

"Sydney, we know of your war record and your close contact with Lionel," one of them said. I protested that it sounded as if he was implying some sort of homosexual relationship, and they said that they had no idea of how a person could feel when facing years of danger together.

"We want you to understand that Commander Crabb's actions were for his country; we would wish you to do the same by identifying the body that you have just examined as that of your Commander."

I queried the request but was assured that it was for my country and that all would later be revealed to me. I never did discover their plan or tactics, nor did I ever change my statement that it was not the body of Commander Crabb, although a lot of pressure was put on me to do so. Indeed, over the years I have felt very angry when I have read wild reports of many journalists that I changed my evidence.

I was asked if I thought the head and hands, which could have provided conclusive identification, had been removed deliberately. My answer was no, I had seen many human bodies and animal parts during my many years of diving and recognised at once that this was a natural occurrence, caused by sea creatures, fish, prawns, crabs, etc, feeding on flesh that was exposed to them, and also the large amount of movement as storms, tides and currents would drag the body over the seabed.

I was contacted again by Mrs Pat Rose, who I knew was engaged to be married to Commander Crabb, and I visited her in her London flat. I found her in a dreadful state and drinking heavily; she was very angry with me for refusing to partner the Commander and said that he was very disappointed that I had broken up our diving partnership of years which had been so successful on so many dives together, including the *Sverdlov* job. She was convinced that he was in Russia and that he would contact her soon. She was sat in a chair and sobbing as I left, her knees covered by a Royal Navy officer's overcoat.

Pat Rose.

On Tuesday June 11th Mr Bridgman opened the inquest. He had received the pathologist's report which stated there was no way of establishing identification. The Admiralty had sent Lieutenant McLanachan from HMS *Vernon* to Chichester police station to assist with identification of the body, but what evidence could be obtained from a man who was a torpedo officer and had never dived with Crabb is a mystery but he was unable to identify the frogman's suit, flippers and underclothes. Later, Lieutenant McLanachan and I had a conversation reminiscing on the time we had spent together in Italy at the Villa Banti in Leghorn.

Crabb's ex-wife had also failed to identify the body. Mr Bridgman concluded that unless the clothing or the body were positively identified, the body may never be recognised by the authorities as that of Commander Crabb and he would not issue a death certificate while identification remained possible. There was no mention of me and nor was I informed about this inquest. The only evidence given before the hearing was adjourned until June 26th was that of the coroner's officer, a P.C. Castleden, who had been to the mortuary with Mr Bridgman to view the body and clothes. This inquest lasted less than an hour and no evidence was given by anyone about the last days of Commander Crabb's life.

On June 14th, Dr King returned to the mortuary and examined the body again, this time reporting a scar "left side, left knee, an inverted Y" and a round scar on the left thigh. It was stated that a number of photographs were also taken but they were never produced as evidence.

On Wednesday June 26th the inquest was resumed and this time I was called to give evidence along with Dr King, Commander Crabb's ex-wife Margaret Elaine Crabb, John Randall, who had found the body, PC Williams, who went to the scene when the body was brought ashore, DS Alan Hoare of the Sussex Constabulary, who was in charge of enquires connected to the body, Amy Thomas, manageress of Commander Crabb's flat in Hans Road, George William Bostock, a temporary clerical officer sent by the Admiralty, plus a number of other people whose names I can no longer recall.

Mrs Margaret Elaine Crabb stated that she had married Commander Crabb on March 15th 1952 and they had lived together until April 1953, when she began proceedings for a divorce, which she obtained in December 1954. She went on to describe his physical appearance, but said she could not identify the body as being that of her ex-husband. John Randal gave evidence of finding the body in the sea. He said that he had been fishing with two friends when he saw an object floating in the water. On reaching it he discovered that it was a man's body in a frogman's suit.

Mr Bostock, the temporary clerical officer from the Admiralty, was the only Royal Navy witness and he was only there to provide Commander Crabb's service history. I was very surprised at the lack of support that the navy gave to the enquiry. Amy Thomas stated that Commander Crabb had been a tenant in one of her flats in London on and off for some five years. Early in April 1956 he had told her he would be going away on business and a few days after that, on Tuesday April 17th 1956, he left and never returned. PC Williams stated that at about 12 noon on June 9th 1957 he was called to the Royal Air Force Station at Thorney Island and, along with the station medical officer, he went to Pilsey Island where they saw some human remains, clothed in a frogman's suit. The head and hands were missing.

I was called and gave evidence about my Naval Service and my years diving together with Commander Crabb. I explained how he had come to have a scar on the side of his left knee, the result of an injury whilst we were diving together under an American Liberty ship freighter in Leghorn harbour Italy in 1944. I also stated that I had been in close contact with him after the war on several dives and was familiar with the clothing he wore when diving because we helped each other to dress and he always wore a two-piece Italian rubber suit with a neck seal and cumber band and he also had two sets of combination underwear – one khaki, one blue – and blue socks and maroon shorts. I also gave evidence that he did not have hammer toes as stated by his wife. His feet were quite normal and in a good condition.

I was then dismissed but I protested in a raised voice that I had not been asked anything more, considering the knowledge I had of Commander Crabb. The bench stated "The court orders you to be silent, Mr Knowles."

Dr King was called to give evidence of his findings. He had already stated on June 10th that he could not find any scars or identifying marks, but now he stated that on June 14th, only four days later, he had returned to the mortuary and examined the remains again, this time reporting that he had found a scar "left side of left knee, an inverted Y," and also another one on the left thigh, about the size of an old sixpence, which had been caused by a seawater boil. A photograph had been taken in his presence of the scar but was never shown in evidence.

Why did the coroner not question the fact that in the original report there had been no mention of any scars on the lower part of the body (which was true) but then suddenly, like magic, they had appeared in the evidence? Did my drawings that I had given to the CID in Preston Police Station of the exact location of the scars have any bearing on this new report? It was glaringly clear to me that these new scars had been "created" and that Dr King had been intimidated into adding this new material to his testimony.

I again attempted to intervene but was silenced when the coroner's clerk raised his arm and the palm of his hand.

The whole inquest lasted less than an hour. In private I asked Mr Bridgman if it would be possible for me to examine the body again. His reply was a curt, "Contact the police; your request is now outside my jurisdiction." And with a shrug he dismissed me.

In court I felt that the right questions were not being asked and to people who obviously knew little or nothing about Commander Crabb. Also questions were asked that certain people could not answer. I felt that apart from me, everyone had been primed and the whole inquest had become a travesty. I tried to speak with the Chief Inspector, who I had reported to at the mortuary, to request another visit and examination of the body, but he was never available.

The coroner recorded an open verdict, as it was impossible to determine the cause of death and based upon the evidence provided a death certificate was issued on June 28th 1957 stating that the cause of death was "NOT ASCERTAINABLE P.M." In my opinion this contradictory evidence should have been examined by a High Court judge and I am sure that the verdict would have been vastly different from that of the Chichester one.

On Friday July 5th 1957, the body of the unknown man was buried at Milton Cemetery, Portsmouth. I did not attend. Mrs Beatrice Crabb, the Commander's mother, attended and she later told me that in her heart she did not believe it was the grave of her son, but she could not let the other poor man go alone

Some six months previously, in November 1956, a Mr Harry Cole had been out fishing in Emsworth harbour near Chichester. It was dark and he was fishing alone when he felt an obstruction on his trawl line and on hauling it to the surface he discovered a large object enclosed in rubber. He struggled to hold it and to his horror in the dim light realised it was a body wearing breathing apparatus. Being alone, the weight was too much for him to hold and the breathing pipe that he was grasping broke away and the body sank back into the depths. He reported the incident to the police on February 7th 1957, stating that he had found the body round about November 3rd 1956, but because of the long time delay in Cole reporting the incident and the many strong and fast tides that flowed through that area, police dismissed it as useless to investigate. He stated to the police that the only thing he could recall after searching his memory was that the body was wearing a fawn coloured rubber suit, surrounded in the middle by a black cumber band, but he could not be certain because the light was bad.

Nobody seemed to care about the important significance of this first discovery of a body (eight months before the body I examined in the mortuary) nor was the news of the find released to the general public nor was this fact raised at the inquest. It seems incredible that the police never investigated, as both the navy and police were supposed to be searching for the body of Commander Crabb. Or was anyone interested in carrying out a search?

UNANSWERED QUESTIONS

1.) **Why did the operation take place in daylight?** A covert operation such as this would always be carried out under the cover of darkness, as were the Italian operations in Gibraltar and the spying mission under the Russian cruiser, *Sverdlov*, previously carried out successfully by Commander Crabb and myself.

2.) **How many divers were involved?** One theory has it that there were four divers, three of whom supposedly returned. Where this 'information' came from I do not know, neither do I believe it. The story that three other Royal Navy divers accompanied Commander Crabb to the *Ordzhonikidze* I believe to be a figment of someone's vivid imagination, as an action of this type would certainly have attracted attention.

3.) **Was there a practise dive?** Another story documented in the official report is that Commander Crabb, on the early evening of April 18th, executed a practice dive and entered the water from a small boat in broad daylight. Why? This would also have attracted attention, owing to this action being within sight of the Russians. Can these reports be true? I think not. As we had already carried out a similar successful operation under the *Sverdlov*, why change the format for a much more dangerous one? It is incomprehensible to me that these actions took place and had I been with the Commander they certainly would not have done so.

4.) **Why was he abandoned?** If he was on a secret mission, why was no attempt made to search for him, even after the Russians had departed, for with his weighted diving gear his body would be lying in a known area.

5.) **Where was his buddy diver?** When I declined to go with him on this mission he had informed me that he had been provided with another buddy diver and that they had been training together secretly in a lake in Wales and that he was "very, very good". I suspected that he was a member of the SBS (Special Boat Squad) and a Royal Marine. No experienced diver dives alone. It is reported that Commander Crabb was dressed for his last dive from the small boat by a Lieutenant Commander Franklin, who was never called to the mortuary to identify the Commander's diving gear, nor was he called to the inquest.

6.) **It was reported that the Commander went to HMS Vernon to pick up diving gear and an oxygen cylinder. Why?** His preferred Italian gear could be carried in a small handbag and the cylinder also would have been small, not like the scuba gear of today. The dual cylinders of the Italian Gruppa Gamma diving gear used by the Commander and myself were approximately 30cm x 10cm but could be singled up. I also doubt that a diver could have navigated his way across the murky waters of Portsmouth harbour completely submerged to arrive secretly under the cruiser and a man of Commander Crabb's vast diving experience would have been well aware of this.

7.) **Why is the official report still being censored?** I have in my possession Sir Edward Bridges' Top Secret Report to the Prime Minister relating to the circumstances in which Commander Crabb undertook an intelligence operation against the Russian warships in Portsmouth harbour, released under the Freedom of Information Act 2000. This report also mentions the work carried out by Commander Crabb and me under the Russian cruiser *Sverdlov* when she visited Portsmouth in October 1955. The report, now available to the public, is almost unreadable; pages 11 to 17 are missing and most of the others to a great degree are blanked out.[15]

8.) **Who or which department sanctioned the operation and ignored the Prime Minister's order?** On April 6th 1956 the First Lord asked the Prime Minister for authority to carry out an operation against the Russian warships. On April 12th the Prime Minister minutes to the First Lord of the Admiralty to inform him that the intelligence operation, now codenamed "CLARET", could not go ahead. The Foreign Office was also aware of this decision. The recently-released papers give no new information at all as to who requested the operation, the Admiralty thinking it was the Foreign Office and vice-versa.

9.) **Why was Harry Cole, who discovered the first body, not called to give evidence at the inquest?** Was the first body found by Harry Cole the body of Commander Crabb? I believe it was, because the body I examined in the mortuary was definitely *not* the Commander's. The brief description of the diving suit given to the police by Harry Cole was enough to convince me that the body he pulled from the depths in Emsworth harbour in October 1956 was that of Commander Crabb, for he never wore any other type of diving suit than this, with the distinctive black rubber band around the middle. This answered the question for me, for we had dressed

[15] The recently released (October 2007) MOD papers contain nothing more than copies of memos between themselves, the Cabinet Office and David Darlow, a BBC television producer who was requesting permission to produce a documentary about the Commander Crabb/*Ordzhonikidze* affair. The official line is that nothing should be released without the approval of the Cabinet Office and the FCO. In the meantime they remain unavailable on the grounds of intelligence and personal sensitivity and will not go to the Public Records Office until 2032. A poignant footnote to these memos was the comment that by the time of their release "many of us will be beyond caring".

each other hundreds of times during our diving years together.

MY OWN THEORY OF EVENTS

Many thousands of words have been written on the subject of the disappearance of Commander Crabb and many authors are of the opinion that he did, in fact, defect to Russia. Although this makes a jolly good read, this is not my opinion. I assisted Marshall Pugh with many facts to help him finish his book *Commander Crabb* and later Bernard Hutton with his book *Commander Crabb is Alive* the preface to which I wrote but was later to find 'the facts' had been distorted to make a novel more than a true story.

It is also reported that Crabb was shot by a Russian sniper when seen on the surface, but the sound of a rifle shot would have been heard clearly and nothing was ever reported by the continuous watch-keepers on the Royal Navy vessels moored in the harbour very close by.

As I have stated previously, Commander Crabb and I were diving partners for many years and were very firm friends, a friendship forged by trust, danger and the mutual love of our work. Inevitably we confided in each other on many issues. When he invited me to go with him to the meetings at the house in Tite Street for the 'Last Suppers' I sensed he was becoming enmeshed in the dark and sinister world of espionage and politics. I could understand the attraction, as he felt that he was no longer needed by the British Royal Navy, but as a 'dive-a-holic' he needed the excitement of that work and if another country wanted and needed his expertise I really believed he would go.

I must admit that all that was going on around us excited me very much also, but thankfully I kept a level head. He proposed to me that we should go to work in Russia and fully expected me to go with him. He seemed to be living in some fantasy world and had no idea that this was, for him, a British hero, impossible, plus the fact that he had been employed by the British Navy in secret experimental work which the British would not like the Russians to obtain.

My objections to this crazy idea led to us having some very heated arguments, but he persisted in saying that he would go. As I could see how serious the outcome would be if he was to go ahead with his plans, I struggled with my conscience. Should I stay loyal to my friend and Commander or should I inform the powers that be of his intentions?

After much soul searching I decided that my loyalty to the country that I loved and had served faithfully for many years under many hazardous conditions must come first. After meeting Alistair Malcolm from MI5 I felt more at ease when he told that they were well aware of Commander Crabb's intentions and that he would be stopped from going to Russia, although he would not go into details.

When the Commander approached me to join him on the dive under the *Ordzhonikidze* I 'smelt a rat', for to my mind there was no sound reason to do this as we had found out in our dive together all that was needed to be known about the moving ability of the Russian cruisers from our dive under the *Sverdlov* only five months earlier. To my mind this was a red-herring to get the Commander into the water and then say that he had died while on unofficial operations.

My personal belief is that his so-called 'buddy' diver was a member of the Special Boat Squad (SBS), a Royal Marine specialist, waiting for him underwater with instructions to kill him, and I seriously think that they fought and killed each other. This would explain the two bodies later being found; the first in Oct 1956 and the second in June 1957.

Even with all my years of underwater work I would have never tackled my boss in that situation, for he was like an eel, but I feel that he met his match on that occasion and it resulted in both men dying.

To my mind there could be no more fitting end to Commander Lionel Crabb than this.

His final "Ten Minutes of Hell".

Commander Crabb's medals.

Lionel Crabb's gravestone at Milton Cemetery, Portsmouth, erected by his mother, Beatrice, although the true identity of the body buried there remains in doubt.

Postscript

Over fifty years have gone by since Commander Crabb disappeared and I have missed him terribly and experienced a great deal of torment. Emotional scars cannot be seen but I do carry them. I have been particularly distressed over the years by the many sly and occasionally blatant insinuations put forward by some commentators that I, along with MI5/6, was somehow involved in his disappearance.

In 1986 I retired and along with my wife, Joan, I decided to spend the rest of my life in Spain. We chose the beautiful little town of Calpe, situated on the East coast. The adjacent rock is a copy in miniature of Gibraltar, which made me feel at home, but all the roads in the town proved too steep for my wife – she had not been in good health for some months – so we decided to move south to Torremolinos. Just eight months later she died suddenly and was interred in the British Cemetery in the city of Malaga, set in a beautiful garden on a steep hillside overlooking the Mediterranean.

One day I was contacted by the authors Mike and Jacqui Welham, who were in the process of writing a book about the disappearance of Commander Crabb; they asked me to assist them, which I was happy to do. I went to visit them at their home in Norfolk and their book was published in 1990 under the title *Frogman Spy*. We met in London and booked into a hotel near to the airport. Mike Welham had sought the assistance of a security company, headed by Gary Murray (a second dan black belt) to act as our minder.

During the night Mike's car was broken into and some of his documents strewn on the floor.

I later returned to my home in Spain and continued to give them some further assistance by telephone, as and when required. Both Mike Welham and I were of the opinion that our telephones were being tapped. One morning in April 1990 I was walking into the town accompanied by the my neighbour, Maria Dolores Crespo, whose husband, Colonel Crespo, is a serving officer in the Spanish army. As I stepped onto the pedestrian crossing adjacent to the Hotel Cervantes, a yellow van veered around the corner of the building, accelerating to a high speed and heading directly towards me. I immediately grasped that the intention was to knock me down and I threw myself backwards and fell to the ground. The van then screeched to a halt and went into reverse in another attempt to do me harm, but by this time I had managed to roll clear. I am in no doubt that my speedy reactions saved my life.

My neighbour, Maria Dolores, was screaming in fright throughout the incident, as were other surprised witnesses. But then a man leapt from the van, bent over me and, grasping my shoulders, shook me violently and shouted in English, "You have said enough, understand, *enough*!" He threw me back on to the ground and ran back to the van, which roared off up the street.

Maria Dolores insisted that the incident was reported to the Spanish police, which it was, but the officer just took a few notes and shrugged his shoulders, because neither we nor any of the other witnesses had taken the registration number of the van and therefore there was nothing they could do. This incident left me very shaken and for months afterwards I was forever looking over my shoulder and occasionally still do so. Colonel Crespo insisted that I went with his wife to a lawyer's office and we made a sworn affidavit in the event that anything should happen to me in the future.

I am still living in Spain, not too far from Gibraltar, where all those years ago my Commander and friend started a new and exciting life for me with its unbelievable adventures. A number of years later I was remarried, by the mayor of our little village in the mountains of Andalusia, to my wonderful and beautiful wife Frances. I will be forever grateful to her for her patience and for constantly giving my memory a jog – and also for all the hours she has spent at the keyboard.

In November 2007 a story emerged from Russia when a Russian ex-frogman claimed that he had killed Commander Crabb. Eduard Koltov told a Russian documentary team that he killed Crabb while investigating suspicious activity under the *Ordzhonikidze.* He stated that he saw a silhouette of a diver in a light frogman suit who was fiddling with something at the starboard end of the ship, next to the ship's ammunition stores and when he swam closer he saw that the frogman was fixing a mine to the ship. He claims that he cut the diver's throat with a knife.

Having watched the interview with Koltov and seeing the supposed knife, which in my opinion looked new and more like a hunting knife than a diver's knife of that era (I myself own an original diver's knife) I concluded that this was a man looking for his fifteen minutes of fame and a few roubles.

I was contacted by the BBC for my opinion about this claim. I dismissed it as unthinkable that anyone would have been ordered to undertake such a task, as the outcome could have resulted in a war with Russia. The Cold War was just beginning to thaw at that time. It is true that Commander Crabb and I had examined the Russian cruiser *Sverdlov* only six months before, but our instructions were to examine the ship and discover the means of her remarkable manoeuvrability and nothing more.

No doubt in the future I shall be contacted to give my opinion on other wild claims that surface and I shall answer to the best of my knowledge without any lies or fabrications.

I have hated reading so many books by authors, articles by journalists and statements by people who had never met my Commander, who have wildly exaggerated the facts, added a lot of fiction and turned them into novels that contain little or no substance.

The writing of my memoirs has taken me back to my roots: to the days of my childhood, both happy and sad; to the early days during the Second World War when I saw so much death and suffering, and remembering some of these events has brought tears to my eyes. Then to my meeting with Commander Crabb and the influence that meeting was to have on the remainder of my life, the many adventures we had together and the friendship and comradeship we shared. This for me has been a traumatic journey, with my emotions running high.

Only time will tell if my assumptions concerning the mysterious disappearance of Commander Lionel Kenneth Philip Crabb, RNVR, GM, OBE are correct, but unfortunately I will not be alive to hear them, nor will a lot of my readers.

Sydney James Knowles BEM (military)
Malaga, Spain 2008

Bibliography

Binding, T. (2006). *Man Overboard.* London: Picador.

Hale, D. (2007). *The Final Dive: The Life and Death of Buster Crabb.* London: Sutton.

Hutton, J. B. (1968). *Commander Crabb Is Alive.* London: Tandem.

Pugh, M. (1956). *Commander Crabb.* London: Macmillan.

Welham, M. G., & Welham, J. A. (1990). *Frogman Spy: The Mysterious Disappearance of Commander 'Buster' Crabb.* London: W.H. Allen / Virgin Books.

Index